Working Papers

for

Fundamental Accounting Principles

VOLUME 2 – CHAPTERS 12-25

Twenty-First Edition

John J. Wild
University of Wisconsin—Madison

Ken W. Shaw
University of Missouri—Columbia

Barbara Chiappetta
Nassau Community College

Prepared by

John J. Wild
University of Wisconsin—Madison

McGraw-Hill
Irwin

McGraw-Hill
Irwin

Working Papers for
FUNDAMENTAL ACCOUNTING PRINCIPLES, VOLUME 2 – CHAPTERS 12-25, Twenty-First Edition
John J. Wild, Ken W. Shaw, and Barbara Chiappetta

Published by McGraw-Hill/Irwin, an imprint of The McGraw-Hill Companies, Inc., 1221 Avenue of the
Americas, New York, NY 10020. Copyright © 2013, 2011, 2009, 2007, 2005, 2002, 1999, 1996, 1993, 1990, 1987, 1984, 1981, 1978, 1975,
1972, 1969, 1966, 1963, 1959, and 1955 by The McGraw-Hill Companies, Inc. All rights reserved. Printed in the United States of America.

1 2 3 4 5 6 7 8 9 0 DOW/DOW 1 0 9 8 7 6 5 4 3

ISBN: 978-0-07-752521-7
MHID: 0-07-752521-3

www.mhhe.com

TABLE OF CONTENTS

Chapter

(a) _____

_____

_____

(b) _____

_____

_____

Quick Study 12-2

	Share to _____	Share to _____	Total
Net income			
Salary allowance:			
_____			
_____			
Total salary allowances			
Balance of income			
Balance allocated:			
_____			
_____			
Total allocated			
Balance of income			
Shares of the partners			

Quick Study 12-3

_____

_____

_____

_____

_____

Quick Study 12-4

_____

_____

_____

_____

_____

GENERAL JOURNAL

Date	Account Titles and Explanation	PR	Debit	Credit

Quick Study 12-6

GENERAL JOURNAL

Date	Account Titles and Explanation	PR	Debit	Credit

Quick Study 12-7

(1)

	Field	*Brown*	*Snow*	*Total*
Initial investments				
Allocation of all losses				
Capital balances				

(2)

GENERAL JOURNAL

Date	Account Titles and Explanation	PR	Debit	Credit

(3)

GENERAL JOURNAL

Date	Account Titles and Explanation	PR	Debit	Credit

Quick Study 12-8

_____
_____
_____
_____
_____
_____
_____
_____
_____
_____
_____
_____

	Characteristic	General Partnerships
1.	Life	
2.	Owners' liability	
3.	Legal status	
4.	Tax status of income	
5.	Owners' authority	
6.	Ease of formation	
7.	Transferability of ownership	
8.	Ability to raise large amounts of capital	

Exercise 12-2

Part a

Recommended Organization: _____
_____
_____
_____
_____
_____

Taxation Effects: _____
_____
_____

Advantages: _____
_____
_____
_____

Part b

Recommended Organization: _____

_____

_____

_____

_____

_____

Taxation Effects: _____

_____

_____

Advantages: _____

_____

_____

_____

Part c

Recommended Organization: _____

_____

_____

_____

_____

_____

Taxation Effects: _____

_____

_____

Advantages: _____

_____

_____

_____

(1)

GENERAL JOURNAL

Date	Account Titles and Explanation	PR	Debit	Credit
(a)				
(b)				
(c)				

(2)

Capital account balances:		
Initial investment		
Withdrawals		
Share of income		
Ending balances		

GENERAL JOURNAL

Date	Account Titles and Explanation	PR	Debit	Credit
(1)				
(2)				

Name _____

	Share to _____	Share to _____	Total
(1)			
(2)			
(3)			

Name _____

	Share to _____	Share to _____	Total

(1)

_____

_____

_____

_____

_____

_____

_____

_____

_____

_____

_____

_____

_____

(2)

_____

_____

_____

_____

_____

_____

_____

_____

_____

_____

_____

_____

(1)

GENERAL JOURNAL

Date	Account Titles and Explanation	PR	Debit	Credit

(2)

GENERAL JOURNAL

Date	Account Titles and Explanation	PR	Debit	Credit

(3)

GENERAL JOURNAL

Date	Account Titles and Explanation	PR	Debit	Credit

(1)

GENERAL JOURNAL

Date		Account Titles and Explanation	PR	Debit	Credit

(2)

GENERAL JOURNAL

Date		Account Titles and Explanation	PR	Debit	Credit

(3)

GENERAL JOURNAL

Date		Account Titles and Explanation	PR	Debit	Credit

Exercise 12-9

GENERAL JOURNAL

Date		Account Titles and Explanation	PR	Debit	Credit

Name _____

(a) Loss computation from selling assets: _____

_____

_____

_____

_____

_____

_____

_____

_____

(b) Loss allocation

	_____	_____	_____	*Total*
Capital balance before				
loss liquidation.....................				
Allocation of loss:				
Capital balances after loss............				

(c) Liability to be paid: _____

_____

_____

Chapter 12   Exercise 12-11   *Name* _____

(a) Loss computation from selling assets: _____

_____
_____
_____
_____
_____
_____
_____
_____
_____

(b) Loss and deficit allocation:

			Total
Capital balance before loss.........			
Allocation of loss:			
Capital balances after loss............			
Allocation of _____ deficit to:			
Cash paid by each partner............			

(c) Liability to be paid: _____

_____

Exercise 12-12

_____
_____
_____
_____
_____
_____
_____
_____
_____
_____

GENERAL JOURNAL

Date	Account Titles and Explanation	PR	Debit	Credit
(1)				
(2)				
(3)				

Supporting calculations: _____

_____

_____

_____

_____

_____

_____

_____

_____

_____

_____

_____

_____

_____

Inc./Loss Sharing Plan	YEAR 1		
	Calculations	Partner: _____	Partner: _____
(a)			
(b)			
(c)			
(d)			

Inc./Loss Sharing Plan	YEAR 2		
	Calculations	Partner: _____	Partner: _____
(a)			
(b)			
(c)			
(d)			

Inc./Loss Sharing Plan	YEAR 3		
	Calculations	Partner:	Partner:
(a)			
(b)			
(c)			
(d)			

Supporting Work Space:

Part 1

Inc./Loss Sharing Plan	Calculations	Partner: ___	Partner: ___	Partner: ___	Total for all Partners
(a)					
(b)					
(c)					

Part 2

| | PARTNERSHIP Statement of Partners' Equity For Year Ended December 31 | | | |
	Partner: _____	Partner: _____	Partner: _____	Partners' Total
Beg. capital balances				
Plus:				
Owner investments				
Net Income:				
Salary allowances				
Interest allowances				
Balance allocated				
Total net income				
Total				
Less partners' withdrawals				
End. capital balances				

Part 3

GENERAL JOURNAL

Date		Account Titles and Explanation	PR	Debit	Credit

Part 1

GENERAL JOURNAL

Date	Account Titles and Explanation	PR	Debit	Credit
(a)				
(b)				
(c)				
(d)				
(e)				

Part 2

GENERAL JOURNAL

Date	Account Titles and Explanation	PR	Debit	Credit
(a)				
(b)				
(c)				

(1)

GENERAL JOURNAL

Date	Account Titles and Explanation	PR	Debit	Credit

(2)

GENERAL JOURNAL

Date	Account Titles and Explanation	PR	Debit	Credit

(3)

GENERAL JOURNAL

Date	Account Titles and Explanation	PR	Debit	Credit

(4)

GENERAL JOURNAL

Date	Account Titles and Explanation	PR	Debit	Credit

(1) _____

_____

_____

_____

_____

_____

_____

_____

_____

_____

_____

_____

_____

_____

_____

_____

(2)   GENERAL JOURNAL

Date	Account Titles and Explanation	PR	Debit	Credit

(3)   GENERAL JOURNAL

Date	Account Titles and Explanation	PR	Debit	Credit

(4) _____

_____

_____

_____

_____

_____

(1) _____

_____

_____

_____

_____

_____

_____

(2) _____

_____

_____

_____

_____

_____

_____

_____

_____

(3) _____

_____

_____

_____

_____

_____

_____

_____

Comparative Analysis—BTN 12-2

(1) _____

_____

_____

(2) _____

_____

_____

(3) _____

_____

_____

_____

(1) Income allocation per original agreement:

	Mobey	Oak	Chesterfield	Total
Salary allowance				
Per patient charges				
Totals				

(2) Income allocation per Chesterfield's proposal:

	Mobey	Oak	Chesterfield	Total
Per patient charges				

(3)

_____
_____
_____
_____
_____
_____
_____
_____
_____
_____
_____

STUDY NOTES
Organizations with Partnership Characteristics

_____
_____
_____
_____
_____
_____
_____
_____
_____
_____
_____
_____
_____
_____
_____
_____
_____
_____
_____
_____
_____
_____
_____
_____
_____
_____
_____
_____
_____
_____
_____
_____
_____
_____
_____
_____
_____
_____
_____
_____
_____
_____
_____
_____

Chapter 12   **Taking It to the Net**   *Name* _____
              BTN 12-5

(1) _____

_____

_____

_____

_____

_____

_____

(2) _____

_____

_____

_____

_____

(3) _____

_____

_____

_____

_____

_____

(1)

Income/Loss Sharing Plan	Calculations	Baker	Warner	Rice	Total
(a)					
(b)					
(c)					
(d)					

(2) Team members share solutions.

(3) _____

Chapter 12   **Entrepreneurial Decision**   *Name* _____
                BTN 12-7

(1) _____

_____

_____

_____

_____

_____

_____

(2) _____

_____

_____

_____

(3) _____

_____

_____

_____

_____

_____

Global Decision—BTN 12-8

(1) _____

_____

_____

(2) _____

_____

_____

(3) _____

_____

_____

_____

_____

_____

_____

_____

_____

True Statements: _____

_____

_____

Quick Study 13-2

GENERAL JOURNAL

Date		Account Titles and Explanation	PR	Debit	Credit
(a)					
(b)					

Quick Study 13-3

GENERAL JOURNAL

Date		Account Titles and Explanation	PR	Debit	Credit
(a)					
(b)					

GENERAL JOURNAL

Date		Account Titles and Explanation	PR	Debit	Credit
(a)					
(b)					

Quick Study 13-5

GENERAL JOURNAL

Date		Account Titles and Explanation	PR	Debit	Credit
(a)					
(b)					
(c)					

Quick Study 13-6
(1)

GENERAL JOURNAL

Date		Account Titles and Explanation	PR	Debit	Credit

(2) _____

_____

_____

_____

GENERAL JOURNAL

Date	Account Titles and Explanation	PR	Debit	Credit

Quick Study 13-8

_____ **Company**

Stockholders' Equity

April 2 (after stock dividend)

Quick Study 13-9

Cash Dividend to Common Shareholders

GENERAL JOURNAL

Date	Account Titles and Explanation	PR	Debit	Credit

Quick Study 13-11

(1) _____

_____

_____

_____

(2) _____

_____

_____

_____

Quick Study 13-12

Basic Earnings Per Share _____

_____

_____

_____

_____

Quick Study 13-13

Basic Earnings Per Share _____

_____

_____

_____

_____

Price-Earnings Ratio _____

_____

_____

_____

Analysis _____

_____

_____

_____

Quick Study 13-15

Dividend Yield _____

_____

_____

Analysis _____

_____

_____

_____

Quick Study 13-16

_____

_____

_____

_____

_____

_____

_____

Quick Study 13-17

GENERAL JOURNAL

Date		Account Titles and Explanation	PR	Debit	Credit

Name _____

	Characteristic	Corporations
1	Owner authority & control	
2	Ease of formation	
3	Transferability of ownership	
4	Ability to raise large amounts of capital	
5	Duration of Life	
6	Owner liability	
7	Legal status	
8	Tax status of income	

Exercise 13-2

GENERAL JOURNAL

Date	Account Titles and Explanation	PR	Debit	Credit
(1)				
(2)				
(3)				

Name _____

GENERAL JOURNAL

Date	Account Titles and Explanation	PR	Debit	Credit
(1)				
(2)				
(3)				
(4)				

GENERAL JOURNAL

Date	Account Titles and Explanation	PR	Debit	Credit

Exercise 13-5

(1) _____   (4) _____
(2) _____   (5) _____
(3) _____   (6) _____

Name _____

Part 1
(a) Retained Earnings:

_____
_____
_____
_____

(b) Total Stockholders' Equity:

_____
_____
_____
_____
_____

(c) Number of Outstanding Shares:

_____
_____
_____
_____

Part 2
(a) Retained Earnings:

_____
_____
_____
_____

(b) Total Stockholders' Equity:

_____
_____
_____
_____

(c) Number of Outstanding Shares:

_____
_____
_____
_____

Part 3

_____
_____
_____
_____
_____

Part 1

GENERAL JOURNAL

Date		Account Titles and Explanation	PR	Debit	Credit

Part 2

	Before	After

Part 3

	Feb. 5	Feb. 28

	Non-Cumulative Preferred	Common
2013:		
2014:		
2015:		
2016:		
Totals:		

Exercise 13-9

	Cumulative Preferred	Common
2013:		
2014:		
2015:		
2016:		
Totals:		

Name _____

Part 1

GENERAL JOURNAL

Date	Account Titles and Explanation	PR	Debit	Credit

Name _____

Part 2

Changes to the equity section include: _____

_____
_____
_____
_____
_____
_____
_____
_____
_____
_____
_____
_____
_____
_____
_____
_____
_____
_____
_____
_____
_____
_____
_____

Revised Stockholders' Equity Section (for support of your part 2 solution):

Name _____

_____ **COMPANY**
_____
Statement of Retained Earnings
For Year Ended December 31, 2013
_____

_____
_____
_____
_____
_____
_____
_____
_____
_____
_____
_____

Exercise 13-12

(1) Net Income Available to Common Stockholders: _____

_____
_____
_____
_____
_____

(2) Basic Earnings per Share: _____

_____
_____
_____
_____
_____

(1) Net Income Available to Common Stockholders: _____

_____

_____

_____

_____

_____

(2) Basic Earnings per Share: _____

_____

_____

_____

_____

_____

Exercise 13-14
Price-Earnings Ratio:
(1) _____

(2) _____

(3) _____

(4) _____

Analysis: _____

_____

_____

Exercise 13-15
Dividend Yield:
(1) _____

(2) _____

(3) _____

(4) _____

_____

_____

Analysis: _____

_____

_____

(1)

_____

_____

_____

_____

_____

_____

_____

_____

_____

_____

(2)

_____

_____

_____

_____

_____

_____

_____

_____

_____

_____

_____

Exercise 13-17

(1)

_____

_____

_____

_____

(2)   GENERAL JOURNAL

Date	Account Titles and Explanation	PR	Debit	Credit

(3)

_____

_____

_____

_____

(1)

GENERAL JOURNAL

Date	Account Titles and Explanation	PR	Debit	Credit

(2)

_____ CORPORATION
Statement of Retained Earnings
For Year Ended December 31, 2014

_____

_____

_____

_____

_____

_____

_____

_____

_____

(3)

_____ CORPORATION
Stockholders' Equity Section of the Balance Sheet
December 31, 2014

_____

_____

_____

_____

_____

_____

Part 1

(a) _____
_____

(b) _____
_____

(c) _____
_____

(d) _____
_____

Part 2
Number of Outstanding Shares: _____
_____
_____
_____
_____
_____

Part 3
Minimum Legal Capital: _____
_____

Part 4
Total Paid-In Capital from Common Stockholders: _____
_____
_____
_____
_____
_____

Part 5
Book Value Per Common Share: _____
_____
_____
_____

Part 1

GENERAL JOURNAL

Date	Account Titles and Explanation	PR	Debit	Credit

Part 2

	CORPORATION
	Statement of Retained Earnings
	For Year Ended December 31, 2014

Part 3

	CORPORATION
	Stockholders' Equity Section of the Balance Sheet
	December 31, 2014

Chapter 13   Problem 13-3A or 13-3B   *Name* _____

Part 1

	Explanations for each of the entries:
Oct. 2 (Jan.17)*	
Oct 25 (Feb. 5)*	
Oct. 31 (Feb. 28)*	
Nov. 5 (Mar. 14)*	
Dec. 1 (Mar. 25)*	
Dec. 31 (Mar. 31)*	

* Dates for Problem 13-3B are in parentheses.

Part 2

	Oct. 2 (Jan. 17)*	Oct. 25 (Feb. 5)*	Oct. 31 (Feb. 28)*	Nov. 5 (Mar. 14)*	Dec. 1 (Mar. 25)*	Dec. 31 (Mar. 31)*
Common stock……...……						
Common stock dividend distributable..						
Paid-In capital in excess of par…….....….						
Retained earnings…........						
Total equity……........…….						

*Dates for Problem 13-3B are in parentheses.

Part 1

Outstanding Common Shares: _____

_____

_____

_____

_____

_____

_____

Part 2
Cash Dividend Amounts: _____

_____

_____

_____

_____

_____

Part 3
Capitalization of Retained Earnings: _____

_____

_____

_____

_____

_____

Part 4
Cost Per Share of Treasury Stock: _____

_____

_____

_____

_____

Part 5
Net Income Computation: _____

_____

_____

_____

_____

_____

_____

_____

_____

(1) Market Price Per Share: _____

_____

_____

_____

(2) Computation of Stock Par Values: _____

_____

_____

_____

_____

_____

(3) Book Value Per Preferred Share: _____

_____

_____

   Book Value Per Common Share: _____

_____

_____

_____

_____

_____

(4) Book Value Per Preferred Share: _____

_____

_____

_____

_____

   Book Value Per Common Share: _____

_____

_____

_____

_____

_____

_____

_____

(5) Book Value Per Preferred Share:

_____
_____
_____
_____
_____
_____

Book Value Per Common Share:

_____
_____
_____
_____
_____
_____
_____
_____

(6) _____

_____
_____
_____
_____
_____
_____
_____
_____

(7) _____

_____
_____
_____
_____
_____
_____

(1a)   GENERAL JOURNAL

Date	Account Titles and Explanation	PR	Debit	Credit

(1b)   GENERAL JOURNAL

Date	Account Titles and Explanation	PR	Debit	Credit

(1c)   GENERAL JOURNAL

Date	Account Titles and Explanation	PR	Debit	Credit

(2)   **(a)** _____

(b) _____

(c) _____

(3) _____

(1) _____
_____
_____
_____
_____
_____
_____
_____

(2) _____
_____
_____
_____
_____
_____
_____

(3) _____
_____
_____
_____
_____

(4) _____
_____
_____
_____
_____
_____

(5) _____
_____
_____
_____

(6) FastForward: _____
_____
_____
_____
_____

(1)
Polaris Book Value Per Common Share: _____
_____

Arctic Cat Book Value Per Common Share: _____
_____
_____

(2)
Polaris Earnings Per Share: _____
_____

Arctic Cat Earnings per Share: _____
_____
_____

(3)
Polaris Dividend Yield: _____
_____

Arctic Cat Dividend Yield: _____
_____
_____

Analysis: _____
_____
_____

(4)
Polaris Price-Earnings Ratio: _____
_____

Arctic Cat Price-Earnings Ratio: _____
_____
_____

Analysis & Interpretation: _____
_____
_____
_____

(1) _____

_____
_____
_____
_____
_____
_____
_____
_____
_____
_____
_____
_____
_____
_____
_____
_____
_____
_____
_____
_____
_____
_____
_____
_____
_____
_____
_____
_____
_____
_____
_____
_____
_____
_____
_____
_____

MEMORANDUM

TO:
FROM:
DATE:
SUBJECT:

Company	Earnings Per Share	Market Price of Stock	Price-Earnings Ratio

Industry Norm:

Meaning of Price-Earnings Ratio:

Comparison Across Companies:

Concluding Analysis:

Part 1

_____
_____
_____

Part 2

_____
_____
_____
_____

Part 3

_____
_____
_____
_____

Part 4

_____
_____
_____
_____

Teamwork in Action
BTN 13-6

Part 1
(a) Impact on Financial Position due to Stock Buyback: _____
_____
_____
_____
_____
_____
_____

(b) Reasons for Stock Buyback: _____
_____
_____
_____
_____
_____
_____

GENERAL JOURNAL

Date	Account Titles and Explanation	PR	Debit	Credit
Reacquisition entry				
(a)				
(b)				
(c)				
(d)				
(e)				

Part 3
Similarities: _____
_____
_____

Differences: _____
_____
_____
_____

Part 1

	Plan A	Plan B

Part 2

	Plan A	Plan B

Part 3

_____
_____
_____
_____
_____
_____
_____
_____
_____
_____
_____
_____

Global Decision—BTN 13-9

(1) Book Value per Common Share _____

_____
_____
_____
_____
_____
_____

(2) Earnings per Share _____

_____
_____
_____
_____
_____
_____

(3) Analysis _____

_____
_____
_____
_____
_____

(1) Cash Proceeds: _____
_____

(2) Total Bond Interest Expense: _____
_____
_____
_____
_____

(3) Bond Interest Expense on 1st Payment Date: _____
_____
_____

Quick Study 14-2[B]

(1) Cash Proceeds: _____
_____

(2) Total Bond Interest Expense: _____
_____
_____
_____
_____

(3) Bond Interest Expense on 1st Payment Date: _____
_____
_____

GENERAL JOURNAL

Date		Account Titles and Explanation	PR	Debit	Credit

Quick Study 14-4

(a) _____

_____

_____

_____

_____

_____

_____

_____

_____

_____

(b) _____

_____

_____

_____

_____

_____

_____

_____

Date		Account Titles and Explanation	PR	Debit	Credit
(a)					
(b)					
(c)					

GENERAL JOURNAL

Date	Account Titles and Explanation	PR	Debit	Credit

Quick Study 14-7

GENERAL JOURNAL

Date	Account Titles and Explanation	PR	Debit	Credit

Quick Study 14-8

1. ____ Registered bond
2. ____ Serial bond
3. ____ Secured bond
4. ____ Bearer bond
5. _____ Convertible bond
6. _____ Bond indenture
7. _____ Sinking fund bond
8. _____ Debenture

(a) _____

_____

(b) _____

_____

(c) _____

_____

_____

Quick Study 14-10

Ratio Computations: _____

_____

_____

_____

_____

_____

Analysis and Interpretation: _____

_____

_____

_____

_____

Quick Study 14-11[C]

GENERAL JOURNAL

Date	Account Titles and Explanation	PR	Debit	Credit

GENERAL JOURNAL

Date	Account Titles and Explanation	PR	Debit	Credit

Quick Study 14-13^D

GENERAL JOURNAL

Date	Account Titles and Explanation	PR	Debit	Credit

Quick Study 14-14

(a) _____

_____

(b) _____

_____

_____

Quick Study 14-15

(a) _____

_____

_____

(b) _____

_____

_____

(c) _____

_____

_____

(d) _____

_____

_____

(1) _____

_____

_____

_____

(2)

GENERAL JOURNAL

Date		Account Titles and Explanation	PR	Debit	Credit
(a)					
(b)					
(c)					

(3)

GENERAL JOURNAL

Date		Account Titles and Explanation	PR	Debit	Credit
(a)					
(b)					

(1) _____

_____

_____

_____

(2) Total Bond Interest Expense: _____

_____

_____

_____

_____

_____

_____

_____

_____

(3) Straight-Line Amortization Table

Semiannual Period-End	Unamortized Discount	Carrying Value
1/01/2013		
6/30/2013		
12/31/2013		
6/30/2014		
12/31/2014		
6/30/2015		
12/31/2015		

Chapter 14   Exercise 14-3^{B} *Name* _____

(1) _____
_____
_____
_____
_____

(2) Total Bond Interest Expense: _____
_____
_____
_____
_____
_____
_____
_____
_____
_____
_____

(3) Effective Interest Amortization Table

Semiannual Interest Period-End	(A) Cash Interest Paid (4.5% x $500,000)	(B) Bond Interest Expense [6% x Prior (E)]	(C) Discount Amortization [(B) – (A)]	(D) Unamortized Discount [Prior (D) – (C)]	(E) Carrying Value [$500,000–(D)]
1/01/2013					
6/30/2013					
12/31/2013					
6/30/2014					
12/31/2014					
6/30/2015					
12/31/2015					

(1) _____
_____
_____
_____
_____

(2) Total Bond Interest Expense: _____
_____
_____
_____
_____
_____
_____
_____
_____

(3) Straight-Line Amortization Table

Semiannual Period-End	Unamortized Premium	Carrying Value
1/01/2013		
6/30/2013		
12/31/2013		
6/30/2014		
12/31/2014		
6/30/2015		
12/31/2015		

(1) _____
_____
_____
_____
_____

(2) Total Bond Interest Expense:
_____
_____
_____
_____
_____
_____
_____
_____
_____

(3) Effective Interest Amortization Table

Semiannual Interest Period-End	(A) Cash Interest Paid [6.5% x $400,000]	(B) Bond Interest Expense [6% x Prior (E)]	(C) Premium Amortization [(A) – (B)]	(D) Unamortized Premium [Prior (D) – (C)]	(E) Carrying Value [$400,000+(D)]
1/01/2013					
6/30/2013					
12/31/2013					
6/30/2014					
12/31/2014					
6/30/2015					
12/31/2015					

Date		Account Titles and Explanation	PR	Debit	Credit
(a)					
(b)					
(c)					

Date		Account Titles and Explanation	PR	Debit	Credit
(a)					
(b)					
(c)					

Name _____

Date		Account Titles and Explanation	PR	Debit	Credit
(a)					
(b)					
(c)					

(1) Semiannual Cash Interest Payment:

_____

_____

_____

_____

(2) Number of Payments:

_____

_____

_____

(3) _____

_____

_____

_____

(4) Market Price Computation:

_____

_____

_____

_____

_____

_____

_____

(5)

GENERAL JOURNAL

Date	Account Titles and Explanation	PR	Debit	Credit

Name _____

(1) Semiannual Cash Interest Payment:

_____
_____
_____
_____

(2) Number of Payments:

_____
_____
_____
_____

(3)

_____
_____
_____
_____

(4) Market Price Computation:

_____
_____
_____
_____
_____
_____

(5)

GENERAL JOURNAL

Date	Account Titles and Explanation	PR	Debit	Credit

(1) Cash proceeds from sale: _____

_____

_____

(2) Discount at issuance: _____

_____

_____

_____

(3) Total Amortization for First 6 Years: _____

_____

_____

_____

_____

(4) Carrying value of the bonds at 12/31/2018: _____

_____

_____

_____

_____

_____

_____

(5) Purchase price: _____

_____

_____

(6) Loss on retirement: _____

_____

_____

_____

_____

(7)   **GENERAL JOURNAL**

Date	Account Titles and Explanation	PR	Debit	Credit

(1) _____

_____

_____

_____

_____

(2)   **GENERAL JOURNAL**

Date	Account Titles and Explanation	PR	Debit	Credit

(1) Straight-Line Amortization Table

Semiannual Period-End	Unamortized Discount	Carrying Value
6/01/2013		
11/30/2013		
5/31/2014		
11/30/2014		
5/31/2015		
11/30/2015		
5/31/2016		
11/30/2016		
5/31/2017		

Supporting computations:

_____
_____
_____
_____
_____
_____
_____
_____
_____

(2)   GENERAL JOURNAL

Date	Account Titles and Explanation	PR	Debit	Credit

(1) Amount of Each Payment: _____

_____

_____

_____

(2)

Period Ending Date	(A) Beginning Balance [Prior (E)]	(B) Debit Interest Expense [7% x (A)]	+	(C) Debit Notes Payable [(D) - (B)]	=	(D) Credit Cash [computed]	(E) Ending Balance [(A) - (C)]
			Payments				
2013							
2014							
2015							
2016							

Name _____

GENERAL JOURNAL

Date	Account Titles and Explanation	PR	Debit	Credit

Name _____

(1)(a) _____

_____

_____

_____

(b) _____

_____

_____

_____

_____

(2) _____

_____

_____

_____

_____

_____

_____

_____

_____

Exercise 14-17[D]

(1) _____

(2) _____

(3) _____

GENERAL JOURNAL

Date		Account Titles and Explanation	PR	Debit	Credit
(1)					
(2)					

Exercise 14-19^D

_____
_____
_____
_____
_____
_____
_____
_____
_____
_____
_____
_____
_____
_____

GENERAL JOURNAL

Date	Account Titles and Explanation	PR	Debit	Credit
(1)				
(2)				

(3) _____

_____

_____

_____

(4) _____

_____

_____

_____

Part 1

(a)

Cash Flow	PV Table Value	Amount	Present Value

(b)

GENERAL JOURNAL

Date		Account Titles and Explanation	PR	Debit	Credit

Part 2

(a)

Cash Flow	PV Table Value	Amount	Present Value

(b)

GENERAL JOURNAL

Date		Account Titles and Explanation	PR	Debit	Credit

Part 3

(a)

Cash Flow	PV Table Value	Amount	Present Value

(b)

GENERAL JOURNAL

Date	Account Titles and Explanation	PR	Debit	Credit

Problem 14-2A or 14-2B

Part 1

GENERAL JOURNAL

Date	Account Titles and Explanation	PR	Debit	Credit

Part 2

(a) Cash Payment: _____
_____
_____

(b) Semiannual Amortization: _____
_____
_____
_____

(c) Bond Interest Expense: _____
_____
_____

Part 3

Total Bond Interest Expense: _____
_____
_____
_____
_____
_____
_____
_____
_____
_____

Part 4 Straight-Line Amortization Table

Semiannual Period-End	Unamortized Discount	Carrying Value
1/01/2013		
6/30/2013		
12/31/2013		
6/30/2014		
12/31/2014		

Part 5

GENERAL JOURNAL

Date	Account Titles and Explanation	PR	Debit	Credit

Problem 14-3A or 14-3B

Part 1

GENERAL JOURNAL

Date	Account Titles and Explanation	PR	Debit	Credit

Part 2

(a) Cash Payment: _____

_____

(b) Semiannual Amortization: _____

_____

_____

(c) Bond Interest Expense: _____

_____

_____

Total Bond Interest Expense: _____

_____

_____

_____

_____

_____

_____

_____

_____

_____

_____

Part 4 Straight-Line Amortization Table

Semiannual Period-End	Unamortized Premium	Carrying Value
1/01/2013		
6/30/2013		
12/31/2013		
6/30/2014		
12/31/2014		

Part 5

GENERAL JOURNAL

Date	Account Titles and Explanation	PR	Debit	Credit

Part 1

Total Bond Interest Expense: _____

_____

_____

_____

_____

_____

_____

_____

_____

_____

Part 2 Straight-Line Amortization Table

Semiannual Interest Period-End	Unamortized Premium	Carrying Value
1/01/2013		
6/30/2013		
12/31/2013		
6/30/2014		
12/31/2014		
6/30/2015		
12/31/2015		
6/30/2016		
12/31/2016		
6/30/2017		
12/31/2017		

Part 3

GENERAL JOURNAL

Date		Account Titles and Explanation	PR	Debit	Credit

Part 1

Total Bond Interest Expense: _____

_____

_____

_____

_____

_____

_____

_____

_____

_____

Part 2 Effective Interest Amortization Table

Semiannual Interest Period-End	(A) Cash Interest Paid [__% x $____]	(B) Bond Interest Expense [__% x Prior (E)]	(C) Premium Amortization [(A) - (B)]	(D) Unamortized Premium [Prior (D) - (C)]	(E) Carrying Value [$____ + (D)]
1/01/2013					
6/30/2013					
12/31/2013					
6/30/2014					
12/31/2014					
6/30/2015					
12/31/2015					
6/30/2016					
12/31/2016					
6/30/2017					
12/31/2017					

Part 3

GENERAL JOURNAL

Date			PR	Debit	Credit

Part 4

Cash Flow	PV Table Value	Amount	Present Value

Comparison to Part 2 Table:

_____
_____
_____
_____
_____
_____
_____
_____

Part 1

GENERAL JOURNAL

Date	Account Titles and Explanation	PR	Debit	Credit

Part 2

Total Bond Interest Expense:

_____

_____

_____

_____

_____

_____

_____

_____

_____

_____

Part 3   Straight-Line Amortization Table

Semiannual Interest Period-End	Unamortized Discount	Carrying Value
1/01/2013		
6/30/2013		
12/31/2013		
6/30/2014		
12/31/2014		

Part 4

GENERAL JOURNAL

Date	Account Titles and Explanation	PR	Debit	Credit

Part 5 (for Problem 14-6A only)

_____
_____
_____
_____
_____
_____
_____
_____
_____
_____
_____
_____
_____
_____
_____
_____
_____
_____
_____
_____
_____
_____

Part 1

GENERAL JOURNAL

Date	Account Titles and Explanation	PR	Debit	Credit

Part 2

Total Bond Interest Expense: _____

_____

_____

_____

_____

_____

_____

_____

_____

_____

_____

Part 3 Effective Interest Amortization Table

Semiannual Interest Period-End	(A) Cash Interest Paid [__% x $__]	(B) Bond Interest Expense [__% x Prior (E)]	(C) Discount Amortization [(B) - (A)]	(D) Unamortized Discount [Prior (D) - (C)]	(E) Carrying Value [$____ - (D)]
1/01/2013					
6/30/2013					
12/31/2013					
6/30/2014					
12/31/2014					

Part 4

GENERAL JOURNAL

Date	Account Titles and Explanation	PR	Debit	Credit

Part 1

GENERAL JOURNAL

Date	Account Titles and Explanation	PR	Debit	Credit

Part 2

Total Bond Interest Expense: _____

_____

_____

_____

_____

_____

_____

_____

_____

_____

Part 3 Effective Interest Amortization Table

Semiannual Interest Period-End	(A) Cash Interest Paid [__% x $___]	(B) Bond Interest Expense [__% x Prior (E)]	(C) Premium Amortization [(A) - (B)]	(D) Unamortized Premium [Prior (D) - (C)]	(E) Carrying Value [$____ + (D)]
1/01/2013					
6/30/2013					
12/31/2013					
6/30/2014					
12/31/2014					

Part 4

GENERAL JOURNAL

Date	Account Titles and Explanation	PR	Debit	Credit

Part 5

GENERAL JOURNAL

Date	Account Titles and Explanation	PR	Debit	Credit

Part 6

_____
_____
_____
_____
_____
_____
_____
_____
_____
_____
_____
_____
_____
_____

Part 1

Amount of Each Payment: _____

_____

_____

_____

_____

_____

_____

_____

Part 2

Period Ending Date	(A) Beginning Balance [Prior (E)]	Payments			(E) Ending Balance [(A) - (C)]
		(B) Debit Interest Expense + [___% x (A)]	(C) Debit Notes Payable = [(D) - (B)]	(D) Credit Cash [computed]	

Part 3

GENERAL JOURNAL

Date	Account Titles and Explanation	PR	Debit	Credit

Problem 14-10A or 14-10B

Part 1

_____ **Company—Debt-to-Equity Ratio:** _____

_____

_____

_____

_____

_____

_____ **Company—Debt-to-Equity Ratio:** _____

_____

_____

_____

_____

_____

Part 2

Analysis and Interpretation: _____

_____

_____

_____

_____

_____

_____

Part 1

Present Value of the Lease Payments: _____

_____

_____

_____

Part 2

GENERAL JOURNAL

Date		Account Titles and Explanation	PR	Debit	Credit

Part 3

Capital Lease Liability Payment (Amortization) Schedule:

Period Ending Date	Beginning Balance of Lease Liability	Interest on Lease Liability (__%)	Reduction of Lease Liability	Cash Lease Payment	Ending Balance of Lease Liability
Year 1					
Year 2					
Year 3					
Year 4					
Year 5					

Part 4

GENERAL JOURNAL

Date		Account Titles and Explanation	PR	Debit	Credit

Part 1

Maximum Loan Allowed: _____

_____

_____

_____

_____

_____

_____

_____

_____

_____

_____

_____

_____

Part 2

(a) Percent of Assets Financed by Debt _____

_____

_____

_____

(b) Percent of Assets Financed by Equity _____

_____

_____

_____

Part 3

_____

_____

_____

_____

_____

_____

_____

(1) _____

_____

_____

_____

_____

_____

_____

_____

_____

_____

(2) _____

_____

_____

_____

(3) _____

_____

_____

_____

(4) FastForward: _____

_____

_____

_____

_____

_____

_____

(1) Polaris

       Current Year:

_____

_____

_____

_____

       Prior Year:

_____

_____

_____

_____

Arctic Cat

       Current Year:

_____

_____

_____

_____

       Prior Year:

_____

_____

_____

_____

(2) _____

_____

_____

_____

_____

_____

(1) _____

_____

_____

_____

_____

_____

_____

_____

_____

_____

_____

_____

_____

_____

(2) _____

_____

_____

_____

_____

_____

_____

_____

_____

_____

MEMORANDUM
TO: FROM: DATE: SUBJECT:

(1) Long Term Liabilities:

_____

_____

_____

_____

_____

_____

_____

_____

(2a)

_____

_____

_____

_____

_____

(2b)

_____

_____

_____

_____

_____

_____

Parts 1 and 2

_____
_____
_____
_____
_____
_____
_____
_____
_____
_____
_____
_____
_____
_____
_____
_____
_____
_____
_____
_____
_____
_____
_____

Part 3

_____
_____
_____
_____
_____
_____
_____
_____
_____

Part 4

_____
_____
_____
_____
_____
_____

Part 5

Similarities	Differences

Part 1

	Current	Alternative Notes for Expansion				
		10% Note	15% Note	16% Note	17% Note	20% Note
Income before interest..............						
Interest expense.						
Net income.........						
Equity................						
Return on equity.						

Work Space:

_____

_____

_____

Part 2

_____

_____

_____

_____

_____

_____

_____

_____

_____

_____

_____

_____

_____

_____

_____

_____

_____

_____

_____

_____

_____

_____

Global Decision—BTN 14-9

(1) Current Year Ratio: _____

_____

_____

_____

  Prior Year Ratio: _____

_____

_____

_____

_____

(2) _____

_____

_____

_____

_____

GENERAL JOURNAL

Date	Account Titles and Explanation	PR	Debit	Credit

Quick Study 15-2

(1)

GENERAL JOURNAL

Date	Account Titles and Explanation	PR	Debit	Credit

(2)
_____
_____
_____
_____

(3)

GENERAL JOURNAL

Date	Account Titles and Explanation	PR	Debit	Credit

GENERAL JOURNAL

Date		Account Titles and Explanation	PR	Debit	Credit

Quick Study 15-4

GENERAL JOURNAL

Date		Account Titles and Explanation	PR	Debit	Credit

Quick Study 15-5
True: _____

_____

_____

_____

Quick Study 15-6

(1) _____   (4) _____
(2) _____   (5) _____
(3) _____

GENERAL JOURNAL

Date		Account Titles and Explanation	PR	Debit	Credit

Quick Study 15-8

GENERAL JOURNAL

Date		Account Titles and Explanation	PR	Debit	Credit

Quick Study 15-9

GENERAL JOURNAL

Date		Account Titles and Explanation	PR	Debit	Credit

(1)

GENERAL JOURNAL

Date	Account Titles and Explanation	PR	Debit	Credit

(2) _____
_____
_____
_____
_____

Quick Study 15-11

(1) _____
_____
_____
_____

(2) _____
_____
_____

Quick Study 15-12

Return on Total Assets: _____
_____
_____
_____
_____

Quick Study 15-13

(1) Return on Total Assets—Component Analysis _____
_____
_____
_____
_____

(2) _____
_____
_____
_____
_____

GENERAL JOURNAL

Date	Account Titles and Explanation	PR	Debit	Credit
	Date of Sale:			
	Date of Payment:			

Quick Study 15-15[A]

GENERAL JOURNAL

Date	Account Titles and Explanation	PR	Debit	Credit

Quick Study 15-16

_____

_____

_____

_____

_____

_____

GENERAL JOURNAL

Date		Account Titles and Explanation	PR	Debit	Credit
(a)					
(b)					
(c)					

Exercise 15-2

GENERAL JOURNAL

Date		Account Titles and Explanation	PR	Debit	Credit
(a)					
(b)					

Exercise 15-3

GENERAL JOURNAL

Date		Account Titles and Explanation	PR	Debit	Credit
(a)					
(b)					

(1) _____

(2) _____

(3) _____

(4) _____

_____

Exercise 15-5

(1) _____

_____

(2) _____

_____

(1)   GENERAL JOURNAL

Date	Account Titles and Explanation	PR	Debit	Credit

(2) _____

_____

_____

_____

_____

_____

(3)   GENERAL JOURNAL

Date	Account Titles and Explanation	PR	Debit	Credit

Exercise 15-7

Available-for-Sale Portfolio	Cost	Fair Value	Unrealized Gain (Loss)

GENERAL JOURNAL

Date	Account Titles and Explanation	PR	Debit	Credit

GENERAL JOURNAL

Date	Account Titles and Explanation	PR	Debit	Credit
(a)				
(b)				
(c)				
(d)				
(e)				
(f)				
(g)				

Name _____

GENERAL JOURNAL

Date		Account Titles and Explanation	PR	Debit	Credit

Computation of Fair Value Adjustment:

Securities	Cost	Fair Value	Unrealized Gain (Loss)

Exercise 15-10

GENERAL JOURNAL

Date		Account Titles and Explanation	PR	Debit	Credit

Computation of Fair Value Adjustment:

	12/31/2012	12/31/2013
Cost		
Fair Value		
Gain (Loss)		

Adjustments:

Name _____

GENERAL JOURNAL

Date	Account Titles and Explanation	PR	Debit	Credit
2011:				
2012:				
2013:				
2014:				

Supporting Computations:

Name _____

(1) Classification of Investments

__(a)__ _____

_____

_____

__(b)__ _____

_____

__(c)__ _____

_____

__(d)__ _____

_____

__(e)__ _____

_____

_____

(2)   GENERAL JOURNAL

Date	Account Titles and Explanation	PR	Debit	Credit

Computation of Fair Value Adjustment:

Long-Term AFS Securities	Cost	Fair Value

Name _____

GENERAL JOURNAL

Date	Account Titles and Explanation	PR	Debit	Credit
2013:				
2014:				

Name _____

2013 Return on Total Assets:

_____

_____

_____

2014 Return on Total Assets:

_____

_____

_____

_____

Analysis and Interpretation:

_____

_____

_____

_____

_____

_____

_____

GENERAL JOURNAL

Date	Account Titles and Explanation	PR	Debit	Credit
2013:				
2014:				

Reported on Quarterly Statement Ended June 30, 2013:

_____
_____
_____
_____
_____
_____

Reported on Quarterly Statement Ended September 30, 2013:

_____
_____
_____
_____
_____
_____

Reported on Quarterly Statement Ended December 31, 2013:

_____
_____
_____
_____
_____
_____

Reported on Quarterly Statement Ended March 31, 2014:

_____
_____
_____
_____
_____
_____

Exercise 15-17

(1) _____

_____
_____

(2) _____

_____
_____
_____

Part 1   GENERAL JOURNAL

Date	Account Titles and Explanation	PR	Debit	Credit
2013:				
2014:				

GENERAL JOURNAL

Date	Account Titles and Explanation	PR	Debit	Credit
2015:				

Part 2

Date	Account Titles and Explanation	PR	Debit	Credit

Part 1

GENERAL JOURNAL

Date	Account Titles and Explanation	PR	Debit	Credit

Part 2

	Comparison of Cost and Fair Value for AFS Portfolio			
Security	Computations	Cost	Fair Value	Unrealized Gain (Loss)

Part 3

GENERAL JOURNAL

Date	Account Titles and Explanation	PR	Debit	Credit

Part 4

_____
_____
_____
_____
_____
_____

Part 5
Income Statement: _____
_____
_____
_____

Balance Sheet (Equity Section Only): _____
_____
_____
_____

Part 1

GENERAL JOURNAL

Date	Account Titles and Explanation	PR	Debit	Credit
2013:				

Supporting work:

GENERAL JOURNAL

Date	Account Titles and Explanation	PR	Debit	Credit
2014:				

Supporting work:

GENERAL JOURNAL

Date	Account Titles and Explanation	PR	Debit	Credit
2015:				

Supporting work:

	12/31/2013	12/31/2014	12/31/2015
Long-Term AFS Securities (cost)			
Fair Value Adjustment Balance			
Long-Term AFS Securities (Fair Value)			

Part 3

	2013	2014	2015
Realized Gains (Losses)			

Unrealized Gains (Losses) at year-end

Problem 15-4A or 15-4B
Part 1
Balance sheet disclosure:

Supporting work:

AFS Securities on Dec. 31, 2013	Cost	Fair Value

Part 2

GENERAL JOURNAL

Date	Account Titles and Explanation	PR	Debit	Credit

Supporting Computations:

AFS Securities	Cost	Fair Value

Part 3
Disclosures:

Stock Sold	Cost	Sale Value	Realized Gain (Loss)

Chapter 15   Problem 15-5A or 15-5B   *Name* _____

Part 1

GENERAL JOURNAL

Date	Account Titles and Explanation	PR	Debit	Credit
2013:				
2014:				
2015:				

(2) Carrying Value Per Share: _____

_____

_____

_____

_____

(3) Change in Equity: _____

_____

_____

_____

_____

_____

_____

(1)

GENERAL JOURNAL

Date	Account Titles and Explanation	PR	Debit	Credit
2013:				
2014:				
2015:				

(2) Investment Cost Per Share: _____

_____

_____

_____

_____

(3) Change in Equity: _____

_____

_____

_____

_____

_____

_____

Part 1

GENERAL JOURNAL

Date	Account Titles and Explanation	PR	Debit	Credit
2013:				

GENERAL JOURNAL

Date	Account Titles and Explanation	PR	Debit	Credit
2014:				

Part 2

Foreign Exchange Gain (Loss) Reported:

_____
_____
_____
_____
_____
_____

Part 3

_____
_____
_____
_____
_____
_____
_____
_____
_____
_____
_____

Part 1

GENERAL JOURNAL

Date	Account Titles and Explanation	PR	Debit	Credit

Part 2

GENERAL JOURNAL

Date	Account Titles and Explanation	PR	Debit	Credit

(1) _____

_____

_____

_____

(2) _____

_____

_____

_____

_____

_____

_____

_____

_____

_____

_____

(3) _____

_____

_____

_____

_____

(4) _____

_____

_____

_____

_____

(5) Fast Forward: _____

_____

_____

_____

_____

_____

_____

_____

_____

(1)   Polaris's Return on Total Assets:

_____
           Current Year
_____

_____

_____
           Prior Year
_____

_____

_____
       Arctic Cat's Return on Total Assets:
           Current Year
_____

_____

_____
           Prior Year
_____

_____

_____

(2)   Polaris's Component Analysis of Return on Total Assets:

_____
           Current Year
_____

_____

_____
           Prior Year
_____

_____

_____

_____
       Arctic Cat's Component Analysis of Return on Total Assets:
           Current Year
_____

_____

_____
           Prior Year
_____

_____

_____

(3) Current Year Analysis: _____
_____
_____
_____

   Prior Year Analysis:: _____
_____
_____
_____
_____

Ethics Challenge BTN 15-3

(1) _____
_____
_____
_____
_____
_____
_____

(2) _____
_____
_____
_____
_____
_____
_____
_____
_____

(3) _____
_____
_____
_____
_____

MEMORANDUM
TO:
FROM:
DATE:
SUBJECT:

(1) _____

_____

_____

_____

_____

_____

_____

_____

_____

(2) _____

_____

_____

_____

_____

_____

_____

_____

_____

(3) _____

_____

_____

_____

_____

_____

_____

_____

(4) _____

_____

_____

_____

(1)

GENERAL JOURNAL

Date	Account Titles and Explanation	PR	Debit	Credit

(2)

GENERAL JOURNAL

Date	Account Titles and Explanation	PR	Debit	Credit

(3) _____

_____

_____

_____

(1) _____

_____

(2) _____

_____

(3) _____

_____

Global Decision—BTN 15-9

(1) Return on Total Assets:

          Current Year

_____

          Prior Year

_____

      Component Analysis of Return on Total Assets:

          Current Year

_____

          Prior Year

_____

(2) Current Year Analysis:

_____

_____

   Prior Year Analysis:

_____

_____

   Overall:

_____

(1) _____

_____

_____

_____

(2) _____

_____

_____

_____

(3) _____

_____

_____

_____

(4) _____

_____

_____

Quick Study 16-2

(1) _____	**(6)** _____
(2) _____	**(7)** _____
(3) _____	**(8)** _____
(4) _____	**(9)** _____
(5) _____	**(10)** _____

Quick Study 16-3

Cash Flows from Operating Activities _____

_____

_____

_____

_____

_____

_____

_____

_____

_____

_____

_____
_____
_____
_____
_____
_____
_____
_____
_____
_____

Quick Study 16-5
(1) _____
_____
_____
_____

(2) _____
_____
_____
_____
_____
_____
_____
_____

Quick Study 16-6^B

Cash Flow from Operating Activities _____
_____
_____
_____
_____
_____
_____
_____
_____
_____
_____

__Cash Inflow from Asset Sale:__ _____

_____

_____

_____

_____

_____

_____

_____

_____

Quick Study 16-8

(1) Cash Paid for Dividends: _____

_____

_____

_____

_____

(2) Cash Payments toward Notes: _____

_____

_____

_____

_____

_____

Quick Study 16-9

(1) Cash Received from Customer: _____

_____

_____

_____

(2) Net Increase or Decrease in Cash: _____

_____

_____

_____

_____

(1) Cash Paid for Merchandise: _____

_____

_____

_____

(2) Cash Paid for Operating Expenses: _____

_____

_____

_____

Quick Study 16-11^B

Cash Flow from Operating Activities _____

_____

_____

_____

_____

_____

_____

_____

_____

_____

Quick Study 16-12

(1) _____

_____

_____

_____

_____

_____

(2) _____

_____

_____

_____

_____

_____
_____
_____
_____
_____
_____
_____

Quick Study 16-14

Cash Flows from Operating Activities	Case X	Case Y	Case Z

Quick Study 16-15

Investing Activities _____
_____
_____
_____
_____

Quick Study 16-16

Financing Activities _____
_____
_____
_____
_____

_____, Inc.
| **Statement of Cash Flows (Indirect Method)** |
| **For Year Ended June 30, 20___** |

Supporting calculations:

(2) _____

(1) _____

_____

_____

	Cash Flow	U.S. GAAP	IFRS
(2) a.			
b.			
c.			
d.			

Exercise 16-1

		\multicolumn{3}{c}{Statement of Cash Flows}	Noncash Investing & Financing Activities	Not Reported on Statement or in Note
		Operating Activities	Investing Activities	Financing Activities		
a.	Declared and paid a cash dividend.					
b.	Recorded depreciation expense.					
c.	Paid cash to settle long-term note payable.					
d.	Prepaid expenses increased this year.					
e.	Accounts receivable decreased this year.					
f.	Purchased land by issuing stock.					
g.	Paid cash to purchase inventory.					
h.	Sold equipment for cash, yielding a loss.					
i.	Accounts payable decreased this year.					
j.	Income taxes payable increased this year.					

Chapter 16   Exercise 16-2[B]   Name _____

		Statement of Cash Flows			Noncash Investing & Financing Activities	Not Reported on Statement or in Note
		Operating Activities	Investing Activities	Financing Activities		
a	Retired long-term notes payable by issuing stock.					
b.	Paid cash toward accounts payable.					
c.	Sold inventory for cash.					
d.	Paid cash dividend that was declared in a prior period					
e.	Accepted six month note receivable in exchange for plant assets.					
f.	Recorded depreciation expense.					
g.	Paid cash to acquire treasury stock.					
h.	Collected cash from sales.					
i.	Borrowed cash from bank by signing a 9 month note payable.					
j.	Paid cash to purchase patent.					

Cash Flows from Operating Activities

_____
_____
_____
_____
_____
_____
_____
_____
_____
_____
_____
_____
_____
_____
_____
_____

Exercise 16-4

Cash Flow from Operating Activities

_____
_____
_____
_____
_____
_____
_____
_____
_____
_____
_____

Case X

Case Y

Case Z

Cash Flows from Operating Activities

_____
_____
_____
_____
_____
_____
_____
_____
_____
_____
_____
_____

Supporting computations:

Exercise 16-7[B]

Cash Flows from Operating Activities

_____
_____
_____
_____
_____
_____
_____
_____
_____

Supporting computations:

Cash Flows from Investing Activities

Exercise 16-9

Cash Flows for Financing Activities

_____ , Inc.
Statement of Cash Flows (Indirect Method)
For Year Ended June 30, 20___

_____

_____

_____

_____

_____

_____

_____

_____

_____

_____

_____

_____

_____

_____

_____

_____

_____

_____

_____

_____

_____

_____

_____

_____

_____

_____

Supporting Computations for:

(1) Cash received from sale of equipment: _____

_____

_____

_____

_____

Cash paid for new equipment: _____

_____

_____

_____

Part 1

Supporting computations continued.

(2) Cash paid to retire notes: _____

_____

_____

(3) Cash paid for dividends: _____

_____

_____

_____

Part 2

Cash Flow on Total Assets Ratio: _____

_____

_____

Interpretation: _____

_____

_____

_____, Inc.
Statement of Cash Flows (Direct Method)
For Year Ended June 30, 20____

_____

_____

_____

_____

_____

_____

_____

_____

_____

_____

_____

_____

_____

_____

_____

_____

_____

_____

_____

_____

_____

_____

_____

_____

_____

_____

_____

_____

_____

_____

Supporting Computations for:
(1) Cash received from customers:

_____

_____

(2) Cash paid for merchandise inventory:

_____

_____

_____

_____

_____

Part 1

Supporting Computations Continued.

(3) Cash paid for other operating expenses:

_____

_____

_____

(4) Cash paid for income taxes:

_____

_____

(5) Cash received from sale of equipment:

_____

_____

_____

Cash paid for new equipment:

_____

_____

_____

(6) Cash paid to retire notes:

_____

_____

(7) Cash paid for dividends:

_____

_____

_____

Cash Flows from Operating Activities

_____

_____

_____

_____

_____

_____

_____

_____

_____

_____

_____

_____

_____

_____

_____

_____

Exercise 16-13
(1) Cash Flows from Operating Activities

_____

_____

_____

_____

_____

_____

_____

_____

_____

_____

_____

(2) _____

_____

_____

_____

_____

(3) _____

_____

_____

_____

_____

		Spreadsheet for Statement of Cash Flows		
		For Year Ended December 31, 20___		
			Analysis of changes	
	Dec. 31, 2012	*Debit*	*Credit*	*Dec. 31, 2013*

Balance sheet-debit bal. accounts:

Cash...

Accounts receivable........................

Merchandise inventory....................

Plant assets..................................

Balance sheet-credit bal. accounts:

Accum. depreciation-Plant assets

Accounts payable......................

Notes payable..........................

Long-term notes payable..........

Common stock.........................

Retained earnings...................

Statement of cash flows:

Operating activities

Net income...............................

_____ in accts. receivable...

_____ in merch. inventory...

_____ in accounts payable...

Depreciation expense..............

Investing activities

Payment for plant assets..............

Financing activities

Payment of cash dividends.....

Issued note payable...................

_____ **COMPANY**
Statement of Cash Flows
For Year Ended December 31, 20___

_____

_____

_____

_____

_____

_____

_____

_____

_____

_____

_____

_____

_____

_____

_____

_____

_____

_____

_____

_____

_____

_____

_____

_____

_____

_____

Footnotes:

_____

_____

_____

Chapter 16   Exercise 16-16^B   *Name* _____

Part 1

_____ **CORPORATION**
_____

Statement of Cash Flows
_____

For Year Ended December 31, 20___
_____

Part 2

(a) _____

(b) _____

(c) _____

(d) _____

2012 _____

_____

_____

2013 _____

_____

_____

Interpretation:

_____

_____

_____

_____
Statement of Cash Flows
For Year Ended December 31, 20___

Part 1

Statement of Cash Flows
For Year Ended December 31, 20___

_____
_____
_____
_____
_____
_____
_____
_____
_____
_____
_____
_____
_____
_____
_____
_____
_____
_____
_____
_____
_____
_____
_____
_____
_____
_____
_____
_____

Statement Footnotes:

_____
_____
_____

Supporting calculations:

Part 2

_____

_____

_____

_____

_____

_____

_____

_____

_____

_____

_____

_____

Spreadsheet for Statement of Cash Flows
For Year Ended December 31, 20___

	Dec. 31, 2012	Analysis of changes		Dec. 31, 2013
		Debit	Credit	
Balance sheet-debit bal. accounts:				
Cash..				
Accounts receivable......................				
Merchandise inventory...................				
Prepaid expenses.........................				
Equipment....................................				
Balance sheet-credit bal. accounts:				
Accum. depreciation-Equip.......				
Accounts payable....................				
Short-term notes payable.........				
Long-term notes payable..........				
Common Stock, $___par value...				
Paid-in capital in excess of				
par value, common stock.......				
Retained earnings...................				
Statement of cash flows:				
Operating activities				
Net income.............................				
_____ in accts. receivable...				
_____ in merch. inventory...				
_____ in prepaid expenses...				
_____ in accounts payable...				
Depreciation expense..............				
_____ on sale of equipment..				
Investing activities				
Receipt from sale of equipment...				
Payment to purchase equipment..				
Financing activities				
Borrowed on short-term note....				
Payment on long-term note......				
Issued common stock for cash..				
Payments of cash dividends.....				
Noncash investing and financing				
activities:				
Purchase of equip. financed				
by long-term note payable.....				

Statement of Cash Flows
For Year Ended December 31, 20___

Statement Footnotes:

_____

_____

_____

Supporting calculations:

Statement of Cash Flows	
For Year Ended December 31, 20____	

Statement Footnotes:

Supporting calculations:

Statement of Cash Flows
For Year Ended December 31, 20___

_____
_____
_____
_____
_____
_____
_____
_____
_____
_____
_____
_____
_____
_____
_____
_____
_____
_____
_____
_____
_____
_____
_____
_____
_____
_____
_____

Supporting calculations:

| | | Spreadsheet for Statement of Cash Flows | | |
| | | For Year Ended December 31, 20___ | | |

| | | Analysis of changes | | |
	Dec. 31, 2012	Debit	Credit	Dec. 31, 2013
Balance sheet-debit bal. accounts:				
Cash...				
Accounts receivable.........................				
Merchandise inventory......................				
Equipment......................................				
Balance sheet-credit bal. accounts:				
Accum. depreciation-Equip................				
Accounts payable............................				
Income taxes payable......................				
Common stock, $___par value...........				
Paid-in capital in excess of				
par value, common stock............				
Retained earnings..				
Statement of cash flows:				
Operating activities				
Net income...................................				
_____ in accts. receivable..........				
_____ in merch. inventory..........				
_____ in accounts payable.........				
_____ in income taxes payable...				
Depreciation expense....................				
Investing activities				
Payment for equipment....................				
Financing activities				
Issued common stock for cash..........				
Paid cash dividends.........................				

Statement of Cash Flows
For Year Ended December 31, 20___

_____
_____
_____
_____
_____
_____
_____
_____
_____
_____
_____
_____
_____
_____
_____
_____
_____
_____
_____
_____
_____
_____
_____
_____
_____
_____
_____

Supporting calculations:

Statement of Cash Flows
For Year Ended December 31, 20___

Supporting calculations:

Cash Flows from Operating Activities - Indirect Method

_____
_____
_____
_____
_____
_____
_____
_____
_____
_____
_____
_____
_____
_____
_____
_____
_____

Problem 16-8A[B] or 16-8B[B]

Cash Flows from Operating Activities - Direct Method

_____
_____
_____
_____
_____
_____
_____
_____
_____
_____
_____
_____
_____

SUCCESS SYSTEMS	
Statement of Cash Flows	
For Three Months Ended March 31, 20___	

Supporting calculations:

(1) _____

_____

(2) _____

_____

_____

_____

_____

(3) _____

_____

_____

_____

_____

_____

_____

_____

(4) _____

_____

_____

_____

_____

_____

_____

_____

_____

(5) FastForward: _____

_____

_____

_____

_____

_____

_____

_____

(1)   Polaris's Cash Flow on Total Assets Ratio:

       Current Year

_____

_____

       Prior Year

_____

_____

    Arctic Cat's Cash Flow on Total Assets Ratio:

       Current Year

_____

_____

       Prior Year

_____

_____

(2) _____

_____

_____

_____

_____

_____

_____

(3) _____

_____

_____

_____

_____

_____

(4) _____

_____

_____

_____

_____

_____

(1) (a) _____

_____

_____

_____

    (b) _____

_____

_____

_____

_____

_____

_____

(2) _____

_____

_____

_____

_____

_____

_____

_____

_____

_____

_____

_____

_____

MEMORANDUM

TO:
FROM:
DATE:
SUBJECT:

_____
_____
_____
_____
_____
_____
_____
_____
_____
_____
_____
_____
_____
_____
_____
_____
_____
_____
_____
_____
_____
_____
_____
_____
_____
_____
_____
_____
_____
_____
_____
_____
_____
_____
_____
_____
_____
_____
_____
_____
_____

(1) _____
_____
_____
_____

(2) _____
_____
_____

(3)	2010	2011
Net income (net loss)		
Cash flow from operations		

Analysis: _____
_____
_____

(4) _____
_____
_____
_____

(5) _____
_____
_____

(6) _____
_____
_____
_____

Teamwork in Action—BTN 16-6
Part 1

(a) _____
_____
_____
_____
_____

Part 1

(b) Similarities	Differences
_____	_____
_____	_____
_____	_____
_____	_____
_____	_____
_____	_____
_____	_____

(c) _____

_____

_____

_____

_____

_____

_____

_____

_____

(d) _____

_____

_____

_____

_____

_____

_____

_____

_____

Part 2

Adjusting Net Income to Cash Flow from Operating Activities	
Items to Add	**Items to Subtract**
a. _____	_____
b. _____	_____
c. _____	_____
d. _____	_____

Part 3

(a) _____
_____
_____
_____
_____
_____
_____
_____

(b) _____
_____
_____
_____
_____
_____
_____
_____
_____
_____
_____
_____
_____

(c) _____
_____
_____
_____
_____
_____
_____
_____
_____

(d) _____
_____
_____
_____
_____
_____
_____
_____

(1) _____

_____

_____

_____

_____

_____

_____

_____

_____

_____

(2) _____

_____

_____

_____

_____

_____

_____

_____

_____

_____

MEMORANDUM

TO:
FROM:
DATE:
SUBJECT:

(1) _____
_____
_____
_____

(2) _____
_____
_____
_____
_____
_____
_____
_____

(3) _____
_____
_____
_____
_____

Global Decision—BTN 16-10

(1) Cash Flow on Total Assets Ratio _____
   Current Year: _____
_____

   Prior Year: _____
_____
_____
_____

(2) Comparative Analysis: _____
_____
_____
_____
_____
_____

Chapter 17   Quick Study 17-1   *Name* _____

Not part of General-Purpose Statements: _____

_____

_____

_____

_____

Quick Study 17-2

Trend Percents _____

2013	

2012	

Quick Study 17-3
Common-Size Percents _____

2013	

2012	

Quick Study 17-4

Account	2013	2012	Dollar Change	Percent Change

_____
_____
_____
_____
_____
_____
_____
_____
_____
_____
_____
_____
_____
_____
_____
_____
_____
_____
_____
_____
_____
_____
_____
_____

Quick Study 17-6

Ratio	2013	2012	Change
1. Profit Margin Ratio	9%	8%	
2. Debt Ratio	47%	42%	
3. Gross Margin Ratio	34%	46%	
4. Acid-Test Ratio	1.00	1.15	
5. Accounts Receivable Turnover	5.5	6.7	
6. Basic Earnings Per Share	$1.25	$1.10	
7. Inventory Turnover	3.6	3.4	
8. Dividend Yield	2.0%	1.2%	

COMPARATIVE ANALYSIS REPORT

Quick Study 17-8[A]

Name _____

(a) _____

_____

_____

_____

_____

_____

_____

_____

_____

(b) _____

_____

_____

_____

_____

_____

_____

_____

_____

Exercise 17-1

(1) _____	(6) _____
(2) _____	(7) _____
(3) _____	(8) _____
(4) _____	(9) _____
(5) _____	(10) _____

Exercise 17-2

(1) _____

(2) _____

(3) _____

_____

Account	2015	2014	2013	2012	2011

Analysis: _____

_____

_____

_____

_____

_____

_____

Exercise 17-4

Answer: _____

_____

_____

Supporting Work: _____

Name _____

Account	2013	2012

Analysis:

_____

_____

_____

_____

_____

_____

Exercise 17-6

COMPARATIVE ANALYSIS REPORT

_____ Company Common-Size Comparative Balance Sheets December 31, 2012-2014	2014	2013	2012

Analysis and interpretation: _____

(1) Current Ratio:
2014: _____

_____

_____

2013: _____

_____

_____

2012: _____

_____

_____

_____

(2) Acid-test ratio
2014: _____

_____

_____

2013: _____

_____

_____

2012: _____

_____

_____

_____

Analysis and interpretation: _____

_____

_____

_____

_____

_____

_____

_____

1. Days' sales uncollected:

2014: _____

_____

_____

2013: _____

_____

_____

2. Accounts receivable turnover:

2014: _____

_____

2013: _____

_____

_____

3. Inventory turnover:

2014: _____

_____

2013: _____

_____

_____

4. Days' sales in inventory:

2014: _____

_____

2013: _____

_____

Analysis and interpretation: _____

_____

_____

_____

_____

_____

_____

_____

(1)

Debt Ratio and Equity Ratio	2014	2013

(2) Debt-to-Equity Ratio

(3) Times Interest Earned

Analysis and interpretation:

(1) Profit margin:

2014: _____

_____

_____

2013: _____

_____

_____

_____

(2) Total asset turnover:

2014: _____

_____

_____

2013: _____

_____

_____

_____

(3) Return on total assets:

2014: _____

_____

_____

2013: _____

_____

_____

_____

Analysis and interpretation:

_____

_____

_____

_____

_____

_____

_____

_____

Name _____

(1) Return on common stockholders' equity:

2014: _____

_____

_____

_____

2013: _____

_____

_____

_____

(2) Price-earnings ratio, December 31:

2014: _____

_____

_____

2013: _____

_____

_____

(3) Dividend yield:

2014: _____

_____

_____

2013: _____

_____

_____

_____

Analysis and interpretation: _____

_____

_____

_____

_____

_____

_____

_____

_____

(1) _____	(5) _____
(2) _____	(6) _____
(3) _____	(7) _____
(4) _____	(8) _____

Exercise 17-14^A

_____ Merchandising, Inc.
Income Statement
For Year Ended December 31, 20____

Exercise 17-15

1. Current ratio:

Net profit margin

Sales-to-assets:

2.

Part 1   Current Ratio

2014: _____

_____

2013: _____

_____

2012: _____

_____

Part 2

Common-Size Comparative Income Statements For Years Ended December 31, 2014, 2013, and 2012	2014	2013	2012

Part 3

	Balance Sheet Data in Trend Percents December 31, 2014, 2013, and 2012		
	2014	**2013**	**2012**

Part 4

Significant relations revealed: _____

_____

_____

_____

_____

_____

_____

_____

_____

_____

_____

_____

_____

_____

_____

_____

_____

_____

Part 1

| | **Income Statement Trends** | | | | | | |
| | **For Years Ended December 31, 2014–2008** | | | | | | |
	2014	*2013*	*2012*	*2011*	*2010*	*2009*	*2008*

| | **Balance Sheet Trends** | | | | | | |
| | **December 31, 2014–2008** | | | | | | |
	2014	*2013*	*2012*	*2011*	*2010*	*2009*	*2008*

Part 2

Analysis and interpretation: _____

_____

_____

_____

_____

_____

_____

_____

_____

_____

_____

_____

_____

_____

_____

_____

_____

_____

_____

Transaction	Current Assets	Quick Assets	Current Liabilities	Current Ratio	Acid-Test Ratio	Working Capital
Beg. Bal.						
End. Bal.						

Supporting computations:

(1) Current ratio:

_____
_____
_____

(2) Acid-test ratio:

_____
_____
_____

(3) Days' sales uncollected:

_____
_____
_____

(4) Inventory turnover:

_____
_____
_____

(5) Days' sales in inventory:

_____
_____
_____

(6) Debt-to-equity ratio:

_____
_____
_____

(7) Times interest earned:

_____
_____
_____

(8) Profit margin ratio:

_____
_____
_____

(9) Total asset turnover: _____
_____
_____
_____

(10) Return on total assets: _____
_____
_____
_____

(11) Return on common stockholders' equity: _____
_____
_____
_____
_____

Part 1

	Company	*Company*
a. Current ratio:		
b. Acid-test ratio:		
c. Accounts (incl. notes) receivable turnover:		
d. Inventory turnover:		
e. Days' sales in inventory:		
f. Days' sales uncollected:		
Short-term credit risk analysis:		

Part 2

	Company	Company
a. Profit margin ratio:		

b. Total asset turnover:

c. Return on total assets:

d. Return on common stockholders' equity:

e. Price-earnings ratio:

f. Dividend yield:

Investment analysis:

Part 1   Effect of Income Taxes:

Items	Pretax	___% Tax Effect	After-Tax

Part 2 Income from Continuing Operations (and its Components):

_____

_____

_____

_____

_____

_____

_____

_____

_____

_____

_____

_____

_____

_____

_____

_____

_____

_____

_____

Part 3 Income from Discontinued Segment:

_____
_____
_____
_____
_____
_____

Part 4 Income before Extraordinary Items:

_____
_____
_____
_____
_____

Part 5 Net Income:

_____
_____
_____
_____
_____
_____

(1) Gross Margin Ratio (with services revenue):

_____
_____
_____

Gross Margin Ratio (without services revenue):

_____
_____
_____

Profit Margin Ratio:

_____
_____
_____

(2) Current Ratio:

_____
_____
_____

Acid-Test Ratio:

_____
_____
_____

(3) Debt Ratio:

_____
_____
_____

Equity Ratio:

_____
_____
_____

(4) Current Assets as % of Total Assets:

_____
_____
_____

Long-Term Assets as % of Total Assets:

_____
_____
_____

(1) Trend Percents for selected income statement accounts:

	2011	2010	2009
Revenues			
Cost of goods sold			
Operating income			
Non-operating expenses (income)			
Income taxes			
Net income			

(2) Common-size percents for asset categories and accounts:

	2011	2010
Total current assets		
Property and equipment, net		
Goodwill and other intangible assets		

(3) Analysis and Interpretation: _____

_____
_____
_____
_____
_____
_____
_____
_____
_____
_____
_____
_____
_____
_____

(4) FastForward

_____
_____
_____
_____
_____
_____
_____
_____
_____

(1)

Key figures	Polaris		Arctic Cat	
	Percent	Amount	Percent	Amount
Cash and cash equivalents				
Accounts receivable, net				
Inventories				
Retained earnings				
Cost of sales				
Revenues				
Total assets				

(2)
_____
_____
_____
_____
_____
_____

(3)
_____
_____
_____
_____
_____
_____

(4)
_____
_____
_____
_____
_____
_____
_____

(1) _____

_____

_____

_____

_____

_____

_____

_____

_____

_____

_____

_____

(2) _____

_____

_____

_____

_____

_____

_____

_____

_____

_____

_____

_____

_____

_____

_____

_____

_____

MEMORANDUM
TO:
FROM:
DATE:
SUBJECT:

	2010	2011
1. Profit margin ratio		
2. Gross profit ratio		
3. Return on total assets		
4. Return on common stockholders' equity		
5. Basic net income per common share		

Analysis and Interpretation:

Part 1

Part 2

Part 3

(1) _____

_____

_____

_____

_____

(2) _____

_____

_____

(3) _____

_____

_____

_____

(4) _____

_____

_____

_____

_____

(5) _____

_____

_____

_____

(6) _____

_____

_____

_____

_____

Hitting the Road—BTN 17-8

_____

_____

_____

_____

_____

_____

_____

_____

Key Figures	Percent	Amount
Cash and equivalents……….……………		
Accounts receivable, net…………….……		
Inventories…………….………..…………		
Retained earnings………………….….....		
Cost of Sales……….…………….…..……		
Revenues……………….…..………..……		
Total assets……….………..…….………		

(2) Comparisons and comments

_____
_____
_____
_____
_____
_____
_____
_____
_____
_____
_____
_____
_____
_____
_____
_____
_____

Name _____

Answer: _____

_____

Quick Study 18-2

(1) _____ (4) _____

(2) _____ (5) _____

(3) _____

Quick Study 18-3

Answer: _____

_____

Quick Study 18-4

Answer: _____

_____

Quick Study 18-5

(1) _____ (4) _____

(2) _____ (5) _____

(3) _____

Quick Study 18-6

Usual Sequence: _____

_____

_____

_____

_____

_____

_____

_____

_____

_____

_____

_____

Quick Study 18-8

Answer: _____

Supporting work: _____

_____

_____

_____

_____

_____

_____

Quick Study 18-9

_____

_____

_____

_____

_____ Company
Manufacturing Statement
For Year Ended December 31, 20___

_____
_____
_____
_____
_____
_____
_____
_____
_____
_____
_____
_____
_____
_____

Quick Study 18-11

(1) _____   (3) _____
(2) _____   (4) _____

Quick Study 18-12

_____
_____
_____
_____
_____
_____

Quick Study 18-13

_____
_____
_____
_____
_____
_____
_____
_____
_____

Name _____

	Financial Accounting	Managerial Accounting
1. Time dimension		
2. Users and decision makers		
3. Timeliness of information		
4. Purpose of information		
5. Nature of information		
6. Flexibility of practice		
7. Focus of information		

Exercise 18-2

(1) _____usually covers a period of one year.

(2) _____is the process of monitoring planning decisions and evaluating the organization's activities and employees.

(3) _____is the process of setting goals and making plans to achieve them.

(4) _____usually covers a period of 5 to 10 years.

Business Decision	Primary Information Source	
	Managerial	Financial
1. Determine amount of dividends to pay stockholders...		
2. Evaluate a purchasing department's performance......		
3. Report financial performance to board of directors		
4. Estimate product cost for new line of shoes..............		
5. Plan the budget for next quarter...........................		
6. Measure profitability of all individual stores..............		
7. Prepare financial reports according to GAAP............		
8. Determine location and size for a new plant..............		

(1) Cost classifications:

(a) _____	(d) _____
(b) _____	(e) _____
(c) _____	

(2) Purpose(s):

_____

_____

_____

_____

_____

_____

_____

_____

_____

_____

Exercise 18-5

(1)

Product Costs	Cost by Behavior		Cost by Traceability	
	Variable	Fixed	Direct	Indirect
1. Leather cover for soccer balls.......				
2. Annual flat fee paid for office security....................................				
3. Coolants for machinery................				
4. Wages of assembly workers..........				
5. Lace to hold the leather together...				
6. Taxes on factory........................				
7. Machinery depreciation.............				

(2)

_____

_____

_____

_____

_____

_____

_____

Name _____

| | Product Cost | | | | Period Cost | Direct Cost | Indirect Cost |
| | Prime | | Conversion | | | | |
	Direct Materials	Direct Labor	Direct Labor	Overhead			
1. Factory utilities................							
2. Advertising....................							
3. Amortization of patents on factory machine..............							
4. State and federal income taxes							
5. Office supplies used...........							
6. Bad debts expense............							
7. Small tools used...............							
8. Payroll taxes for production supervisor....................							
9. Accident insurance on factory workers..................							
10. Depreciation--Factory building.							
11. Wages to assembly workers...							
12. Direct materials used..........							

(1) Identification: _____

_____

_____

_____

_____

(2)

Company 1
_____Foods
Current Asset Section
December 31, 2013

Company 2
_____Mfg.
Current Asset Section
December 31, 2013

Discussion: _____

_____

_____

_____

_____

		_____ Company	_____ Company
(1) COST OF GOODS MANUFACTURED			

		_____ Company	_____ Company
(2) COST OF GOODS SOLD			

Merchandising Business

Viking Retail	
Partial Income Statement	
For Year Ended December 31, 20____	

Manufacturing Business

Log Homes Manufacturing	
Partial Income Statement	
For Year Ended December 31, 20____	

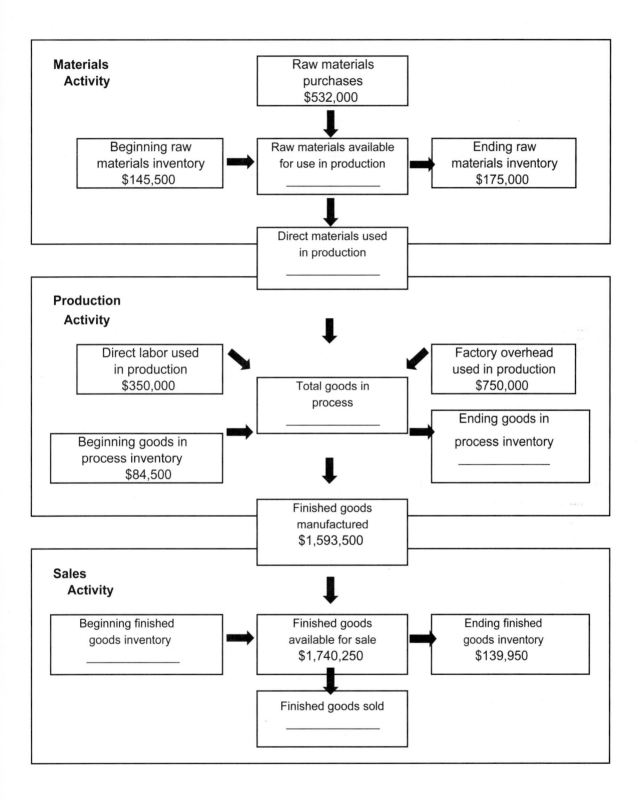

Account	Balance Sheet	Income Statement	Manufacturing Statement	Overhead Report
Accounts receivable………….				
Computer supplies used in office……………………………				
Beginning finished goods inventory………………………				
Beginning goods in process inventory………………………				
Beginning raw materials inventory………………………				
Cash…………………………				
Depreciation expense-Factory building……………………..				
Depreciation expense-Factory equipment……………………				
Depreciation expense-Office building……………………..				
Depreciation expense-Office equipment……………………				
Direct labor…………………….				
Ending finished goods inventory………………………				
Ending goods in process inventory………………………				
Ending raw materials inventory………………………				
Factory maintenance wages..				
Computer supplies used in factory………………………….				
Income taxes…………………				
Insurance on factory building				
Rent cost on office building…				
Office supplies used…………..				
Property taxes on factory building………………………..				
Raw materials purchases……..				
Sales…………………………				

_____Company
Manufacturing Statement
For Year Ended December 31, 20___

_____ Company
Income Statement
For Year Ended December 31, 20___

(1) _____
(2) _____
(3) _____

Exercise 18-15

(a) _____

    (1) _____   (3) _____
    (2) _____   (4) _____

(b) _____
_____
_____
_____
_____
_____

Exercise 18-16

Costs	Cost by Behavior		Cost by Traceability	
	Variable	Fixed	Direct	Indirect
1. Advertising………....………...				
2. Beverage and snacks………...				
3. Regional vice-president salary				
4. Depreciation on ground equipment………………………...				
5. Fuel and oil used in planes…..				
6. Flight attendant salaries………				
7. Pilot salaries…………………….				
8. Ground crew wages……..……..				
9. Tavel agent salaries…………..				

Managerial accounting contributions and responsibilities: _____

_____

_____

_____

_____

_____

_____

_____

_____

_____

_____

_____

_____

_____

_____

_____

Cost Estimation (including opportunity costs): _____

_____

_____

_____

_____

_____

_____

_____

_____

_____

_____

_____

_____

_____

_____

_____

_____

_____

_____

_____

_____

_____

_____

_____

_____

_____

_____

_____

_____

_____

_____

_____

_____

_____

_____

_____

_____

_____

_____

_____

_____

_____

Part 1

Costs	Cost by Behavior		Cost by Function	
	Variable	Fixed	Product	Period
1.				
2.				
3.				
4.				
5.				
6.				
7.				
8.				
9.				
10.				

Part 2

Computation of Manufacturing Cost per _____ For Year Ended December 31, 20___	Total Cost	Per Unit Cost
Variable costs		
Fixed Costs		

Part 3

_____
_____
_____
_____

Part 4

_____
_____
_____
_____

MEMORANDUM

TO:

FROM:

DATE:

SUBJECT: Cost classification and explanation

Part 1

Units and Dollar Amounts for Raw Materials Inventory

_____
_____
_____
_____
_____
_____
_____
_____
_____

Part 2

MEMORANDUM
TO:
FROM:
DATE:
SUBJECT: Consideration of JIT inventory system

Part 1

Merchandising Business

_____
Partial Income Statement
For Year Ended December 31, 20____

Manufacturing Business

_____
Partial Income Statement
For Year Ended December 31, 20____

Part 2

MEMORANDUM
TO:
FROM:
DATE:
SUBJECT: Identifying and reporting inventory accounts

Part 1

_____
Manufacturing Statement
For Year Ended December 31, 20___

Part 2

_____	
Income Statement	
For Year Ended December 31, 20___	

Part 3

Amounts and Inventory Ratios	Raw Materials	Finished Goods

Analysis and discussion:

_____
_____
_____
_____
_____
_____
_____
_____
_____
_____
_____
_____
_____
_____
_____
_____

(1) _____	(6) _____
(2) _____	(7) _____
(3) _____	(8) _____
(4) _____	(9) _____
(5) _____	(10) _____

(1)

Product Costs	Cost by Behavior		Cost by Traceability	
	Variable	Fixed	Direct	Indirect
1. Monthly flat fee to clean workshop.				
2. Laminate coverings for desktops....				
3. Taxes on assembly workshop........				
4. Glue to assemble workstation component parts.....................				
5. Wages of desk assembler.............				
6. Electricity for workshop................				
7. Depreciation on tools...................				

(2)

Success Systems
Manufacturing Statement
For Month Ended January 31, 20____

_____
_____
_____
_____
_____
_____
_____
_____
_____
_____
_____
_____

(3)

Success Systems
Partial Income Statement
For Month Ended January 31, 20____

Cost of goods sold
_____
_____
_____
_____
_____
_____
_____
_____

(1) _____

_____

_____

_____

_____

_____

_____

_____

_____

(2) _____

_____

_____

_____

_____

_____

_____

_____

_____

_____

_____

(3) _____

_____

_____

_____

_____

_____

_____

(4) FastForward: _____

_____

_____

_____

_____

_____

_____

_____

_____

_____

_____

Chapter 18   **Comparative Analysis**
     BTN 18-2
       Name _____

(1) Polaris _____

_____

_____

_____

_____

_____

_____

_____

_____

_____

(2) Arctic Cat _____

_____

_____

_____

_____

_____

_____

_____

(3) _____

_____

_____

_____

_____

_____

_____

_____

(1) Account Identification

_____
_____
_____
_____
_____
_____
_____
_____

(2) CFO Response

_____
_____
_____
_____
_____
_____
_____
_____
_____
_____
_____
_____
_____
_____

MEMORANDUM

TO:

FROM:

DATE:

SUBJECT: Business student salary expectations

(1) Personal Notes from "Statement of Ethical Professional Practice": _____

_____
_____
_____
_____
_____
_____
_____
_____
_____
_____

(2) Overarching Ethical Principles: _____

_____
_____
_____
_____

(3) _____

_____
_____
_____
_____
_____
_____

Attach printout of IMA Ethical Standards

_____

_____

_____

_____

_____

_____

_____

_____

_____

_____

_____

_____

_____

_____

_____

_____

_____

_____

_____

_____

_____

_____

_____

_____

_____

_____

_____

_____

_____

_____

_____

_____

_____

_____

_____

_____

_____

_____

(1) Manufacturing Cost Categories

(a) _____

_____

_____

(b) _____

_____

_____

(c) _____

_____

_____

(2) Total Quality Management

_____

_____

_____

_____

_____

_____

_____

_____

_____

(1) Customer Business Activities (from arrival through departure)

_____
_____
_____
_____
_____
_____

(2) Costs of Customer Business Activities from Part 1

_____
_____
_____
_____
_____
_____
_____
_____

(3) Cost Classification and Explanation

_____
_____
_____
_____
_____
_____
_____

Name _____

(1) Responsibilities

_____

_____

_____

_____

_____

_____

_____

_____

_____

_____

(2) Involvement

_____

_____

_____

_____

_____

_____

_____

_____

_____

_____

_____

Job: _____

Job lot: _____

_____

Quick Study 19-2

_____
_____
_____
_____
_____
_____

Quick Study 19-3

GENERAL JOURNAL

Date	Account Titles and Explanation	PR	Debit	Credit

Quick Study 19-4

GENERAL JOURNAL

Date	Account Titles and Explanation	PR	Debit	Credit

Name _____

GENERAL JOURNAL

Date	Account Titles and Explanation	PR	Debit	Credit

Quick Study 19-6

GENERAL JOURNAL

Date	Account Titles and Explanation	PR	Debit	Credit

Quick Study 19-7

(1) Overhead as Percent of Direct Labor _____

_____

(2) Overhead as Percent of Direct Materials _____

_____

_____

GENERAL JOURNAL

Date	Account Titles and Explanation	PR	Debit	Credit

Computations: _____

_____
_____
_____
_____

Quick Study 19-9

GENERAL JOURNAL

Date	Account Titles and Explanation	PR	Debit	Credit

Computations: _____

_____
_____
_____
_____

Quick Study 19-10

_____
_____
_____
_____
_____

Job Cost Sheet

_____
_____
_____
_____
_____
_____

Quick Study 19-12

_____
_____
_____
_____

Quick Study 19-13

GENERAL JOURNAL

Date	Account Titles and Explanation	PR	Debit	Credit

(1) _____   (5) _____
(2) _____   (6) _____
(3) _____
(4) _____

Exercise 19-2

Job Cost Sheet

_____
_____
_____
_____
_____
_____
_____
_____
_____
_____
_____

Exercise 19-3

(1) _____   (5) _____
(2) _____   (6) _____
(3) _____   (7) _____
(4) _____

Name _____

(1)

_____

_____

_____

_____

_____

_____

_____

_____

(2)

_____

_____

_____

_____

_____

_____

_____

_____

(3)

_____

_____

_____

_____

_____

_____

_____

_____

(4)

_____

_____

_____

_____

_____

_____

_____

(1) Predetermined Overhead Rate _____

_____

_____

(2) _____

_____

_____

_____

_____

_____

Exercise 19-6

(1) Predetermined Overhead Rate _____

_____

_____

(2) _____

_____

_____

_____

_____

_____

(1) Cost of Direct Materials Used

_____
_____
_____
_____
_____
_____
_____
_____

(2) Cost of Direct Labor Used

_____
_____
_____
_____
_____
_____

(3) Cost of Goods Manufactured

_____
_____
_____
_____
_____
_____
_____
_____
_____
_____

(4) Cost of Goods Sold

_____
_____
_____
_____
_____
_____
_____

(5) Gross Profit _____

_____
_____
_____
_____
_____

(6) Overapplied or Underapplied Overhead _____

_____
_____
_____
_____
_____
_____

GENERAL JOURNAL

Date		Account Titles and Explanation	PR	Debit	Credit
(1)					
(2)					
(3)					

Exercise 19-9

GENERAL JOURNAL

Date		Account Titles and Explanation	PR	Debit	Credit
(1)					
(2)					
(3)					

Name _____

GENERAL JOURNAL

Date		Account Titles and Explanation	PR	Debit	Credit
(1)					
(2)					

Exercise 19-11

GENERAL JOURNAL

Date		Account Titles and Explanation	PR	Debit	Credit

Exercise 19-12

GENERAL JOURNAL

Date		Account Titles and Explanation	PR	Debit	Credit
(1)					
(2)					

GENERAL JOURNAL

Date	Account Titles and Explanation	PR	Debit	Credit
(a)				
(b)				
(c)				
(d)				
(e)				
(f)				

GENERAL JOURNAL

Date	Account Titles and Explanation	PR	Debit	Credit
(g)				
(h)				

(1) Predetermined Overhead Rate

_____

_____

_____

_____

_____

_____

_____

(2 & 3)

Overhead

(4)

GENERAL JOURNAL

Date		Account Titles and Explanation	PR	Debit	Credit

(1) Predetermined Overhead Rate _____

_____

_____

_____

_____

_____

_____

(2 & 3)

Overhead

(4)

GENERAL JOURNAL

Date		Account Titles and Explanation	PR	Debit	Credit

(1) Predetermined Overhead Rate _____

_____

_____

_____

(2) Direct Materials Costs

_____

_____

_____

_____

_____

_____

(3) Direct Labor Costs <u>and</u> Overhead Costs _____

_____

_____

_____

_____

_____

_____

_____

_____

_____

_____

_____

Name _____

(1) Predetermined Overhead Rate _____

_____

_____

_____

_____

(2)

	Goods in Process			Finished Goods		
	Cost per Unit	*Units*	*Total Cost*	*Cost per Unit*	*Units*	*Total Cost*
Direct materials						
Direct labor						
Overhead						
Total						

(3) _____

_____

_____

_____

_____

_____

_____

_____

_____

_____

_____

_____

_____

_____

_____

_____

_____

_____

_____

_____

_____

(1) Estimated Cost of the Architectural Job _____

_____

_____

_____

_____

_____

_____

_____

_____

_____

_____

(2) Suggested Bid Price _____

_____

_____

_____

_____

_____

_____

_____

_____

_____

_____

_____

_____

_____

_____

_____

_____

_____

_____

_____

(1)   **GENERAL JOURNAL**

Date		Account Titles and Explanation	PR	Debit	Credit

(2)

_____

_____

_____

_____

Part 1

Total Manufacturing Costs and Costs Assigned to Each Job

Costs	Job_____	Job_____	Job_____	Total for Month

Part 2

GENERAL JOURNAL

Date	Account Titles and Explanation	PR	Debit	Credit
(a)				
(b)				

GENERAL JOURNAL

Date	Account Titles and Explanation	PR	Debit	Credit
(c)				
(d)				
(e)				
(f)				

Part 3

_____
Manufacturing Statement
For Month Ended _____

_____

_____

_____

_____

_____

_____

_____

_____

_____

_____

_____

_____

_____

_____

_____

_____

_____

_____

_____

_____

Part 4

Gross Profit Computation _____

_____
_____
_____
_____
_____
_____

Presentation of Inventories on Balance Sheet _____

_____
_____
_____
_____
_____
_____
_____
_____
_____

Part 5

Impacts of Over- or Underapplied Overhead _____

_____
_____
_____
_____
_____

GENERAL JOURNAL

Date	Account Titles and Explanation	PR	Debit	Credit
(a)				
(b)				
(c)				
(d)				
(e)				

Part 2

GENERAL JOURNAL

Date		Account Titles and Explanation	PR	Debit	Credit

Overhead computations: _____

_____

_____

_____

_____

_____

_____

_____

_____

_____

_____

Part 3

		Debit	Credit
_____			
Trial Balance			
December 31, 20____			

Part 4

	_____
	Income Statement
	For Year Ended December 31, 20____

_____
_____
_____
_____
_____
_____
_____
_____
_____

	_____
	Balance Sheet
	December 31, 20____

_____
_____
_____
_____
_____
_____
_____
_____
_____
_____
_____
_____
_____
_____
_____
_____
_____
_____
_____
_____

Part 5

Error Analysis for Financial Statements

_____
_____
_____
_____
_____
_____
_____

Part 1

JOB COST SHEETS

Job No. _____
Materials........... _____
Labor............... _____
Overhead......... _____
Total Cost........ _____

Job No. _____
Materials......... _____
Labor............... _____
Overhead......... _____
Total Cost........ _____

Job No. _____
Materials......... _____
Labor............... _____
Overhead......... _____
Total Cost........ _____

Job No. _____
Materials......... _____
Labor............... _____
Overhead......... _____
Total Cost........ _____

Job No. _____
Materials......... _____
Labor.............. _____
Overhead......... _____
Total Cost........ _____

Chapter 19   Problem 19-3A or 19-3B   Name _____
            (Continued)
Part 2

GENERAL JOURNAL

Date	Account Titles and Explanation	PR	Debit	Credit
(a)				
(b)				
(c)				
(d)				
(e)				
(f)				
(g)				

GENERAL JOURNAL

Date	Account Titles and Explanation	PR	Debit	Credit
(h)				
(i)				
(j)				

Part 3

GENERAL LEDGER ACCOUNTS

Raw Materials Inventory

Factory Payroll

Goods in Process Inventory

Factory Overhead

Finished Goods Inventory

Cost of Goods Sold

Part 4

Reports of Job Costs
Goods in Process Inventory:
Finished Goods Inventory:
Cost of Goods Sold:

Part 1

(a) Predetermined Overhead Rate _____

_____

_____

_____

_____

(b) Overhead Costs Applied to Jobs

Job No.	Direct Labor	Applied Overhead
_____		
_____		
_____		
_____		
_____		
_____		
Totals..............		

(c) Overapplied or Underapplied Overhead _____

_____

_____

_____

_____

_____

_____

_____

Part 2

GENERAL JOURNAL

Date	Account Titles and Explanation	PR	Debit	Credit

JOB COST SHEET

Customer's Name _____ Company _____ Job No. _____

Direct Materials			Direct Labor			Overhead Costs Applied		
Date	Requisition Number	Amount	Date	Time Ticket Number	Amount	Date	Rate	Amount
						SUMMARY OF COSTS		
						Dir. Materials..		
						Dir. Labor......		
						Overhead......		
Total			Total			Total Cost of the Job........		

JOB COST SHEET

Customer's Name _____ Company _____ Job No. _____

Direct Materials			Direct Labor			Overhead Costs Applied		
Date	Requisition Number	Amount	Date	Time Ticket Number	Amount	Date	Rate	Amount
						SUMMARY OF COSTS		
						Dir. Materials..		
						Dir. Labor......		
						Overhead......		
Total			Total			Total Cost of the Job........		

MATERIALS LEDGER CARD

Item _____

	Received				Issued				Balance		
Date	Receiving Report	Units	Unit Price	Total Price	Requi-sition	Units	Unit Price	Total Price	Units	Unit Price	Total Price

MATERIALS LEDGER CARD

Item _____

	Received				Issued				Balance		
Date	Receiving Report	Units	Unit Price	Total Price	Requi-sition	Units	Unit Price	Total Price	Units	Unit Price	Total Price

MATERIALS LEDGER CARD

Item _____

	Received				Issued				Balance		
Date	Receiving Report	Units	Unit Price	Total Price	Requi-sition	Units	Unit Price	Total Price	Units	Unit Price	Total Price

GENERAL JOURNAL

Date	Account Titles and Explanation	PR	Debit	Credit

(1) Cost of Direct Materials Used in Period for each Job and its Total

_____
_____
_____
_____
_____
_____
_____
_____
_____

(2) Cost of Direct Labor Incurred in Period

_____
_____
_____
_____
_____
_____
_____
_____
_____

(3) Predetermined Overhead Rate for Period

_____
_____
_____
_____
_____
_____
_____
_____
_____

(4) Cost Transferred to Finished Goods Inventory in Period

_____
_____
_____
_____
_____
_____
_____
_____

(1) Costs that will Predictably Increase as a Percent of Sales

_____
_____
_____
_____
_____
_____
_____
_____
_____
_____
_____

(2) Explanation and Performance Assessment of the Costs in Part 1

_____
_____
_____
_____
_____
_____
_____
_____
_____
_____
_____
_____
_____
_____
_____

(3) FastForward:

_____
_____
_____
_____
_____
_____
_____
_____
_____
_____
_____
_____
_____

Part 1

Polaris	Current Year	One Year Prior	Two Years Prior
Inventory change...........			
Operating cash flow effect from inventory change....			

Arctic Cat	Current Year	One Year Prior	Two Years Prior
Inventory change...........			
Operating cash flow effect from inventory change....			

Part 2

Impacts of JIT Inventory System _____

_____

_____

_____

_____

_____

_____

_____

_____

Part 3

Operating Cash Flow Impacts of JIT Inventory System _____

_____

_____

_____

_____

_____

_____

_____

MEMORANDUM

TO:

FROM:

DATE:

SUBJECT: Review of Overhead Allocations

(1) Cost Accounting System Recommendation and Explanation _____

_____
_____
_____
_____
_____
_____
_____
_____
_____
_____
_____
_____
_____

(2) Document Description for Proposed Cost Accounting System _____

_____
_____
_____
_____
_____
_____
_____
_____
_____

(3) Document Facilitation of Cost Accounting System _____

_____
_____
_____
_____
_____
_____
_____
_____
_____
_____
_____
_____

MEMORANDUM

TO:
FROM:
DATE:
SUBJECT: Explanation and recommendation of job order costing software

(1) Appropriateness of Job Order Cost Accounting System _____

_____
_____
_____
_____
_____
_____
_____
_____
_____
_____
_____
_____

(2) Factors Indicative of Job Order System _____

_____
_____
_____
_____
_____
_____
_____
_____
_____
_____
_____
_____

(1) _____

_____

_____

_____

_____

_____

_____

_____

_____

(2) _____

_____

_____

_____

_____

_____

_____

_____

_____

_____

_____

_____

_____

(1)

JOB COST SHEET

Customer's Name _____ Company _____ Job No. _____

	Direct Materials			Direct Labor			Overhead Costs Applied		
Date	Requisition Number	Amount	Date	Time Ticket Number	Amount	Date	Rate	Amount
						SUMMARY OF COSTS		
						Dir. Materials _____		
						Dir. Labor..... _____		
						Overhead..... _____		
Total			Total			Total Cost of		
						the Job........ _____		

Explanation for Overhead Applied: _____

_____

_____

_____

(2) Report Actual Job Cost Sheet and Compare to Your Own in Part 1

Name _____

(1)

KTM ($000s)	Current Year	One Year Prior
Inventory change..		
Operating cash flow effect from inventory change..		

Piaggio (Euro 000s)	Current Year	One Year Prior	Two Years Prior
Inventory change.................			
Operating cash flow effect from inventory change.......			

(2) Implications of JIT Inventory Systems _____

_____

_____

_____

_____

_____

_____

_____

(3) _____

_____

_____

_____

_____

_____

_____

_____

(1) _____
(2) _____
(3) _____
(4) _____

Quick Study 20-2

GENERAL JOURNAL

Date		Account Titles and Explanation	PR	Debit	Credit
(1)					
(2)					

Quick Study 20-3

GENERAL JOURNAL

Date		Account Titles and Explanation	PR	Debit	Credit
(1)					
(2)					

GENERAL JOURNAL

Date	Account Titles and Explanation	PR	Debit	Credit
(1)				
(2)				
(3)				
(4)				

Quick Study 20-5

GENERAL JOURNAL

Date	Account Titles and Explanation	PR	Debit	Credit

Quick Study 20-6

	Equivalent Units
EUP for Labor	

Name _____

The cost of beginning inventory plus the costs added during the period should equal
the cost of units_____ _____plus the cost of _____ _____.

Quick Study 20-8

_____
_____
_____
_____

Quick Study 20-9[A]

EUP for Labor	*Equivalent Units*

Quick Study 20-10

A.	
B.	
C.	
D.	

Name _____

Heading 1: _____
Heading 2: _____
Heading 3: _____

Quick Study 20-12

_____
_____
_____
_____
_____

Quick Study 20-13
1. _____
2. _____
3. _____
4. _____

Quick Study 20-14

EUP for Labor	Equivalent Units

Quick Study 20-15

EUP for Labor	Equivalent Units

(1)	_____	(5)	_____
(2)	_____	(6)	_____
(3)	_____	(7)	_____
(4)	_____		

Exercise 20-2

GENERAL JOURNAL

Date		Account Titles and Explanation	PR	Debit	Credit
1.					
2.					
3.					

Exercise 20-3

GENERAL JOURNAL

Date		Account Titles and Explanation	PR	Debit	Credit
1.					
2.					
3.					

GENERAL JOURNAL

Date	Account Titles and Explanation	PR	Debit	Credit
1.				
2.				

Exercise 20-5

GENERAL JOURNAL

Date	Account Titles and Explanation	PR	Debit	Credit
1.				
2.				

GENERAL JOURNAL

Date	Account Titles and Explanation	PR	Debit	Credit
1.				
2.				
3.				
4.				
5.				

(a) _____

(b) _____

(c) _____

(d) _____

(e) _____

(f) _____

(g) _____

(h) _____

(i) _____

(j) _____

Name _____

(1) Units Transferred to Finished Goods _____

_____

_____

_____

_____

_____

(2)

Equivalent units of production	Direct Materials	Direct Labor

Name _____

1.

Cost per equivalent unit	Direct Materials	Direct Labor

2. Cost Assignment and Reconciliation

Equivalent units of production	Direct Materials	Direct Labor

Exercise 20-11^A

1. Cost per equivalent unit of direct materials and direct labor

	Direct Materials	Direct Labor

Name _____

2. Assignment of costs to output of department

_____

Exercise 20-12

(1)

EUP for Materials

(2)

EUP for Materials

(3) _____

EUP for Materials

_____
_____
_____
_____
_____

Exercise 20-13[A]

(1) _____

EUP for Materials

_____
_____
_____
_____
_____

(2) _____

EUP for Materials

_____
_____
_____
_____
_____

(3) _____

EUP for Materials

_____
_____
_____
_____
_____

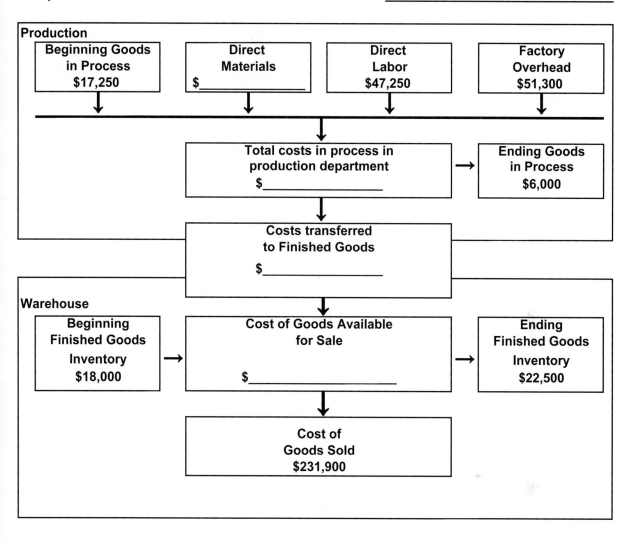

_____COMPANY
Process Cost Summary
For Month Ended _____

Costs Charged to Production

_____

_____

_____

_____

Unit Cost Information

Units to Account For   **Units Accounted For**

_____

_____

_____

_____

_____

Equiv. Units of Production (EUP)	**Direct Materials**	**Direct Labor**	**Factory Overhead**

Cost Per EUP	**Direct Materials**	**Direct Labor**	**Factory Overhead**

Cost Assignment and Reconciliation

_____

_____

_____

_____

_____

_____

_____

_____

_____

_____COMPANY
Process Cost Summary
For Month Ended _____

Costs Charged to Production

_____

_____

_____

_____

<u>Unit Cost Information</u>

Units to Account For   **Units Accounted For**

_____

_____

_____

_____

_____

	Direct	Direct	Factory
Equiv. Units of Production (EUP)	**Materials**	**Labor**	**Overhead**

	Direct	Direct	Factory
Cost Per EUP	**Materials**	**Labor**	**Overhead**

Cost Assignment and Reconciliation

_____

_____

_____

_____

_____

_____

_____

_____

_____

(1)	_____	(7)	_____
(2)	_____	(8)	_____
(3)	_____	(9)	_____
(4)	_____	(10)	_____
(5)	_____	(11)	_____
(6)	_____	(12)	_____

Exercise 20-18

(a)	_____	(e)	_____
(b)	_____	(f)	_____
(c)	_____	(g)	_____
(d)	_____	(h)	_____

Exercise 20-19

Explanation of Hybrid Costing System _____

_____

_____

Product or Service Identification for Hybrid Costing System _____

_____

_____

_____

Name _____

(1) _____

EUP for Materials

_____
_____
_____
_____
_____

(2) _____

EUP for Materials

_____
_____
_____
_____
_____

Exercise 20-21

(1) _____

EUP for Materials

_____
_____
_____
_____
_____

(2) _____

EUP for Materials

_____
_____
_____
_____
_____

_____ COMPANY		
Process Cost Summary		
For Month Ended _____		

Costs Charged to Production

Costs of Beginning work in process

Direct materials...	45000	
Direct Labor...….....	25600	
Factory Overhead..…...	<u>30720</u>	$101,320

Costs incurred this period..		
Direct materials...............................…...................	375000	
Direct Labor........................…..............................	155000	
Factory Overhead ($155,000 x 120%)	(a)_____(b)	_____
Total costs to account for...........................…..............	(c)	_____

<u>Unit Cost Information</u>

Units to Account For		Units Accounted For		
Beginning goods in process...	2,000	Completed & transferred out.......		23,000
Units started this period........	28,000	Ending goods in process.............	(d)	_____
Total units to account for....... (e)	_____	Total units accounted for.............	(f)	_____

Equivalent Units of Production (EUP)	Direct Materials	Direct Labor	Factory Overhead
Units completed and transferred out...	(g)_____ EUP	(h)_____ EUP	(i)_____ EUP
Units of ending goods in process			
Direct materials [(j)_____ x 100%]......	(k)_____ EUP		
Direct labor [(l)_____ x 40%].............		(m)_____ EUP	
Factory overhead [(n)_____ x 40%]....	_____	_____	(o)_____ EUP
Equivalent units of production..........	(p) EUP	(q) EUP	(r) EUP

Cost per EUP	Direct Materials	Direct Labor	Factory Overhead
Costs of beginning goods in process...	$ 45,000	$ 25,600	$30,720
Costs incurred this period..................	375,000	155,000	(s) _____
Total costs...	$ 420,000	$ 180,600	(t) $_____
÷ Equivalent units of production..........	(u) _____	(v) _____	(w) _____
Cost per equivalent unit of production..	(x) $_____ /EUP	(y) $____ /EUP	(z) $_____ /EUP

(continued on next page)

Cost Assignment and Reconciliation

Costs transferred out

Direct materials [(aa)$_____ x (bb)_____]............... (cc) $_____

Direct labor [(dd)$_____ x (ee)_____]..................... (ff)   _____

Factory overhead [(gg)$_____ x (hh)_____].............. (ii)   _____

Total transferred out... (jj) $_____

Cost of ending good in process

Direct materials [(kk)$_____ x (ll)_____].................. (mm) _____

Direct labor [(nn)$_____ x (oo)_____]........................ (pp)   _____

Factory overhead [(qq)$_____ x (rr)_____]................. (ss)   _____

Total ending goods in process.. (tt)   _____

Total costs accounted for.. (uu) $_____

Part 1

Cost of goods transferred and cost of goods sold

_____
_____
_____
_____
_____
_____
_____
_____
_____
_____
_____
_____
_____
_____
_____
_____
_____

Part 2

GENERAL JOURNAL

Date	Account Titles and Explanation	PR	Debit	Credit
a.				
b.				
c.				
d.				

GENERAL JOURNAL

Date	Account Titles and Explanation	PR	Debit	Credit
e.				
f.				
g.				
h.				
i.				
j.				

Part 1 (a and b)

Equivalent units of production	Direct Materials	Direct Labor

Part 2

Costs per equivalent unit	Direct Materials	Direct Labor

Part 3

Assignment of product costs to units

Part 4

MEMORANDUM

TO:

FROM:

DATE:

SUBJECT: Percentage of completion error analysis

_____

_____

_____

_____

_____

_____

_____

_____

_____

_____

_____

_____

_____

_____

_____

_____

_____

_____

_____

_____

_____

_____

_____

_____

_____

_____

_____

_____

_____

Part 1

GENERAL JOURNAL

Date	Account Titles and Explanation	PR	Debit	Credit
a.				
b.				
c.				
d.				
e.				
f.				
g.				
h.				
i.				
j.				

Process Cost Summary
For Month Ended _____

Costs Charged to Production

_____
_____
_____
_____
_____
_____
_____
_____
_____

Unit Cost Information

Units to Account For   **Units Accounted For**

_____
_____
_____
_____

Equiv. Units of Production (EUP)	Direct Materials	Direct Labor	Factory Overhead

Cost per EUP	Direct Materials	Direct Labor	Factory Overhead

Cost Assignment and Reconciliation

_____
_____
_____
_____
_____
_____
_____
_____

Chapter 20   Problem 20-3A or 20-3B   *Name* _____
            (Continued)
Part 3

_____
Impacts of under - or overestimation of the percentage of completion for units in inventory:
_____
_____
_____
_____
_____
_____
_____
_____
_____

Part 1

_____
Process Cost Summary
For Month Ended _____

Costs Charged to Production

_____
_____
_____
_____
_____
_____
_____
_____
_____

Unit Cost Information

Units to Account For   **Units Accounted For**

_____
_____
_____
_____

Equivalent Units of Production (EUP)	Direct Materials	Direct Labor	Factory Overhead

Cost per EUP	Direct Materials	Direct Labor	Factory Overhead

Cost Assignment and Reconciliation

_____
_____
_____
_____
_____
_____
_____
_____
_____
_____

GENERAL JOURNAL

Date	Account Titles and Explanation	PR	Debit	Credit

Part 1

Process Cost Summary
For Month Ended _____

Costs Charged to Production

_____

_____

_____

_____

_____

_____

_____

_____

_____

Unit Cost Information

Units to Account For   **Units Accounted For**

_____

_____

_____

_____

	Direct	Direct	Factory
Equivalent Units of Production (EUP)	**Materials**	**Labor**	**Overhead**

	Direct	Direct	Factory
Cost per EUP	**Materials**	**Labor**	**Overhead**

Process cost summary continued on next page.

Cost Assignment and Reconciliation

_____
_____
_____
_____
_____
_____
_____
_____
_____
_____

Part 2

GENERAL JOURNAL

Date	Account Titles and Explanation	PR	Debit	Credit

Part 3

(a) _____
_____
_____

(b) _____
_____
_____
_____
_____
_____
_____

Part 1

_____
Process Cost Summary
For Month Ended _____

Costs Charged to Production

_____
_____
_____
_____
_____
_____
_____
_____
_____
_____

<u>**Unit Cost Information**</u>

Units to Account For   **Units Accounted For**

_____
_____
_____
_____
_____

Equivalent Units of Production (EUP)	**Direct Materials**	**Direct Labor**	**Factory Overhead**

Cost per EUP	**Direct Materials**	**Direct Labor**	**Factory Overhead**

Process cost summary continued on next page.

Cost Assignment and Reconciliation

_____
_____
_____
_____
_____
_____
_____
_____
_____
_____
_____
_____
_____
_____
_____
_____
_____
_____

Part 2

GENERAL JOURNAL

Date		Account Titles and Explanation	PR	Debit	Credit

(1) Units Transferred to Finished Goods _____

_____

_____

_____

_____

_____

(2) _____

Equivalent units of production	Direct Materials	Direct Labor

(3)

Cost per equivalent unit	Direct Materials	Direct Labor

(4) Cost Assignment and Reconciliation

Part 1

(a and b)

Equivalent units of production	Direct Materials	Direct Labor

Part 2

Costs per equivalent unit	Direct Materials	Direct Labor

Part 3
Assignment of product costs to units

MEMORANDUM

TO:
FROM:
DATE:
SUBJECT: Percentage of completion error analysis

Part 1

_____	
Process Cost Summary	
For Month Ended _____	

Costs Charged to Production

_____

_____

_____

_____

_____

_____

_____

_____

_____

_____

<u>Unit Cost Information</u>

Units to Account For   **Units Accounted For**

_____

_____

_____

_____

_____

Equivalent Units of Production (EUP)	**Direct Materials**	**Direct Labor**	**Factory Overhead**

Cost per EUP	**Direct Materials**	**Direct Labor**	**Factory Overhead**

Process cost summary continued on next page.

Cost Assignment and Reconciliation _____

_____
_____
_____
_____
_____
_____
_____
_____
_____
_____
_____
_____
_____
_____
_____
_____
_____
_____

Part 2

GENERAL JOURNAL

Date	Account Titles and Explanation	PR	Debit	Credit

Part 3

_____
_____
_____
_____
_____

Part 1

Job Order Costing	Process Costing

Part 2

_____

_____

_____

_____

_____

_____

_____

Part 1

[Note: General Ledger accounts shown in Part 4.]
GENERAL JOURNAL

Date	Account Titles and Explanation	PR	Debit	Credit
(a)				
(b)				
(c)				
(d)				
(e)				
(f)				

| Process Cost Summary |
| For Month Ended _____ |

Costs Charged to Production

_____

_____

_____

_____

_____

_____

_____

_____

Unit Cost Information

Units to Account For   **Units Accounted For**

_____

_____

_____

_____

Equivalent Units of Production (EUP)	Direct Materials	Direct Labor	Factory Overhead

Cost per EUP	Direct Materials	Direct Labor	Factory Overhead

Process cost summary continued on next page.

Cost Assignment and Reconciliation

_____
_____
_____
_____
_____
_____
_____
_____
_____
_____
_____
_____
_____

Part 3

GENERAL JOURNAL

Date	Account Titles and Explanation	PR	Debit	Credit
(g)				
(h)				

Part 4

General Ledger accounts:

	Raw Materials Inventory			**ACCOUNT NO. 132**	
Date	**Explanation**	**PR**	**DEBIT**	**CREDIT**	**BALANCE**
June 30	Balance				25,000

	Goods in Process Inventory			**ACCOUNT NO. 133**	
Date	**Explanation**	**PR**	**DEBIT**	**CREDIT**	**BALANCE**
June 30	Balance				8,135

	Finished Goods Inventory			**ACCOUNT NO. 135**	
Date	**Explanation**	**PR**	**DEBIT**	**CREDIT**	**BALANCE**
June 30	Balance				110,000

	Sales			**ACCOUNT NO. 413**	
Date	**Explanation**	**PR**	**DEBIT**	**CREDIT**	**BALANCE**

Cost of Goods Sold				ACCOUNT NO. 502	
Date	Explanation	PR	DEBIT	CREDIT	BALANCE

Factory Payroll				ACCOUNT NO. 530	
Date	Explanation	PR	DEBIT	CREDIT	BALANCE

Factory Overhead				ACCOUNT NO. 540	
Date	Explanation	PR	DEBIT	CREDIT	BALANCE

Part 5
Computation of gross profit for July:

_____

_____

_____

_____

_____

Part 1

_____
_____
_____
_____
_____
_____
_____
_____

Part 2

_____
_____
_____
_____
_____
_____
_____
_____

Part 3 - FastForward:

_____
_____
_____
_____
_____
_____
_____
_____
_____
_____
_____
_____

Chapter 20   Comparative Analysis   Name _____
             BTN 20-2

Part 1

	Polaris		Arctic Cat	
	Current Year	Prior Year	Current Year	Prior Year
COGS/ Total expenses				

Part 2

Analysis and Comparison of Cost Structures: _____

_____

_____

_____

_____

_____

_____

_____

MEMORANDUM

TO:
FROM:
DATE:
SUBJECT: Action plan to understand business processes

MEMORANDUM

TO:
FROM:
DATE:
SUBJECT: Explanation of cost classifications

_____
_____
_____
_____
_____
_____
_____
_____
_____
_____
_____
_____
_____
_____
_____

GENERAL JOURNAL

Date		Account Titles and Explanation	PR	Debit	Credit

(1) _____

_____

_____

_____

_____

_____

_____

_____

_____

_____

_____

_____

_____

(2) _____

_____

_____

_____

_____

_____

_____

_____

_____

(3) _____

_____

_____

_____

_____

_____

_____

_____

Cost description	Direct Materials	Direct Labor	Overhead	Variable cost	Fixed cost

Overhead allocation suggestions:

Name _____

1. Ratio of Cost of Goods Sold to Total Expenses

	Current Year	Prior Year
Piaggio ....…		

	Current Year	Prior Year
Polaris (from BTN 20-2) ….....…..		

	Current Year	Prior Year
Arctic Cat (from BTN 20-2)………....…..…...……		

2. Similarities or Differences Across Years and Companies: _____

_____

_____

_____

_____

_____

_____

_____

Chapter 21   Quick Study 21-1   *Name* _____

Series	Cost behavior
(1)	
(2)	
(3)	
(4)	

Quick Study 21-2

(1) _____	(5) _____
(2) _____	(6) _____
(3) _____	(7) _____
(4) _____	

Quick Study 21-3

Variable Costs: _____

_____

Fixed Costs: _____

_____

_____

_____

(1) Estimated line of cost behavior:

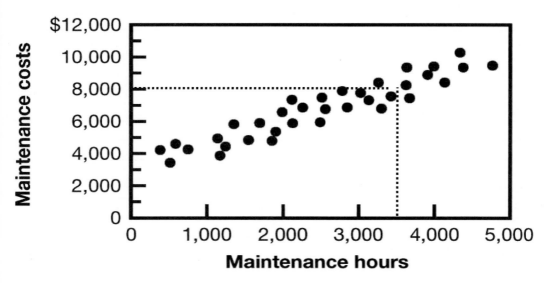

(2) Estimated cost components

   Fixed costs: _____

   Variable costs: _____

_____

_____

Quick Study 21-5

Contribution margin: _____

_____

Contribution margin ratio: _____

_____

Interpretation: _____

_____

_____

Quick Study 21-6

(1) Contribution margin per unit: _____

_____

_____

_____

(2) Break-even point in units: _____

_____

_____

_____

1. _____   4. _____
2. _____   5. _____
3. _____   6. _____

Quick Study 21-8

(1) Contribution margin ratio: _____

_____

_____

(2) Break-even point in dollars: _____

_____

_____

_____

Quick Study 21-9

Units to be Sold to Yield Targeted Net Income _____

_____

_____

_____

_____

_____

_____

_____

Quick Study 21-10

_____

_____

Chapter 21   Quick Study 21-11   *Name* _____

Identification of Company with Higher DOL: _____

Explanation:
_____
_____
_____
_____
_____
_____
_____
_____

Quick Study 21-12

Number and Type Sold at Break-even _____
_____
_____
_____
_____
_____
_____
_____
_____
_____
_____

Quick Study 21-13

Break-even in units: _____
_____

_____
Contribution Margin Income Statement
_____

══
_____
_____
_____
_____
_____
_____
_____

Exercise 21-1

Scatter diagram and estimated line of cost behavior.

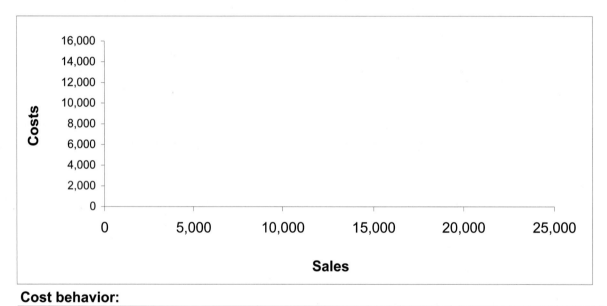

Cost behavior: _____

_____

(1)

Graph	Cost Behavior
(1)	
(2)	
(3)	
(4)	
(5)	

(2)

Cost Item	Graph
(a)	
(b)	
(c)	
(d)	
(e)	

Exercise 21-3

(1)		(4)	
(2)		(5)	
(3)		(6)	

Exercise 21-4

Series	Cost Behavior
(A)	
(B)	
(C)	
(D)	
(E)	

Name _____

(1) Dollar Sales _____

_____

_____

_____

_____

(2) Total Variable Costs _____

_____

_____

_____

_____

_____

Exercise 21-6

Scatter diagram and estimated line of cost behavior.

Cost behavior: _____

_____

SCATTER DIAGRAM METHOD

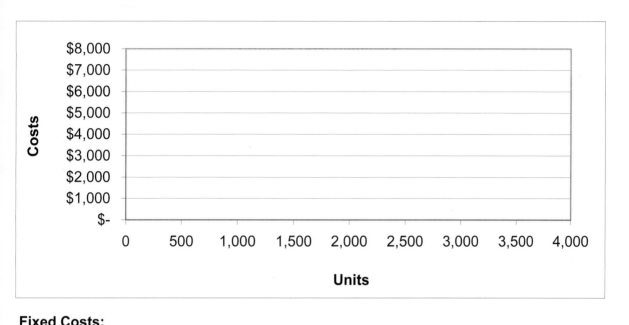

Fixed Costs: _____

_____

_____

Variable Costs per Unit: _____

_____

_____

HIGH-LOW METHOD

Fixed Costs: _____

_____

_____

Variable Costs per Unit: _____

_____

_____

Cost Equation: _____

_____

_____

Fixed Costs: _____

_____

_____

Variable Costs per Unit: _____

_____

_____

Note: Print out and attach Excel output.

Exercise 21-9

(1) Contribution margin: _____

_____

(2) Contribution margin ratio: _____

_____

(3) _____

_____

_____

Chapter 21   Exercise 21-10   *Name* _____

(a) Contribution margin per unit:

_____

_____

(b) Contribution margin ratio:

_____

_____

(c) Break-even point in units:

_____

_____

(d) Break-even point in dollars:

_____

_____

Exercise 21-11

CVP chart:

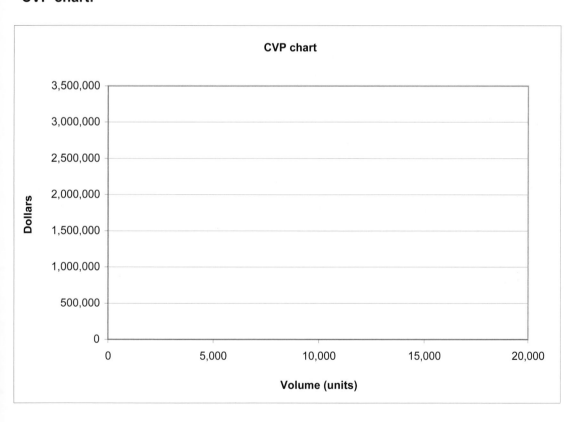

(1)

_____ **COMPANY**

Contribution Margin Income Statement (at Break-Even)

(2)

Sales (in dollars) to break even with increased fixed costs:

(1)   Unit sales at target income

_____

_____

_____

_____

_____

_____

_____

_____

_____

_____

_____

_____

_____

(2)   Dollar sales at target income

_____

_____

_____

_____

_____

_____

_____

_____

_____

_____

_____

Exercise 21-14

_____ **COMPANY**
Forecasted Contribution Margin Income Statement

_____

_____

_____

_____

_____

_____

_____

_____

_____

Name _____

(1) _____

_____

_____

_____

_____

_____

(2) _____

_____

_____

_____

_____

_____

_____

_____

Exercise 21-16

(a) Next Year's Total Expected Variable Costs _____

_____

_____

_____

_____

_____

_____

_____

(b) Next Year's Total Expected Fixed Costs _____

_____

_____

_____

_____

_____

_____

(1) Selling price per composite unit:

_____
_____
_____
_____
_____
_____

(2) Variable costs per composite unit:

_____
_____
_____
_____
_____
_____

(3) Break-even point in composite units:

_____
_____
_____
_____
_____
_____
_____
_____

(4) Unit sales of windows and doors at break-even point:

_____
_____
_____
_____

(1) Weighted-Average Contribution Margin:

_____
_____
_____
_____
_____

(2) Break-Even Point in Units:

_____
_____
_____

(3) Units of Windows and Doors at Break-Even:

_____
_____
_____
_____

Exercise 21-19

(1) Selling Price Per Composite Unit:

_____
_____
_____
_____
_____
_____

(2) Variable Costs Per Composite Unit:

_____
_____
_____
_____
_____
_____

(3) Break-Even Point in Composite Units:

_____
_____
_____
_____
_____
_____

(4) Unit Sales of Each Product at Break-Even:

_____
_____
_____
_____
_____
_____
_____

Exercise 21-20

(1) Weighted-Average Contribution Margin:

_____
_____
_____
_____
_____

(2) Break-Even Point in Units:

_____
_____
_____

(3) Unit Sales of Each Product at Break-Even:

_____
_____
_____
_____
_____

Company A's DOL:

_____

_____

_____

_____

_____

_____

_____

_____

_____

_____

_____

_____

Company B's DOL:

_____

_____

_____

_____

_____

_____

_____

_____

_____

_____

_____

_____

Interpretation:

_____

_____

_____

_____

_____

_____

Parts 1 and 2

_____ Company Contribution Margin Income Statement For Year Ended_____	(_____units)	Per unit	% of sales
Sales..			
Variable costs			
Contribution margin............................			
Fixed costs			
Pretax Income.....................................			
Income tax...			
Net Income..			

Part 3

Analysis _____

_____

_____

_____

_____

_____

_____

Part 1

(a) Break-even point in unit sales: _____

_____
_____
_____
_____
_____
_____
_____
_____

(b) Break-even point in dollar sales: _____

_____
_____
_____
_____
_____
_____
_____
_____
_____

Part 2

Graph for 2A

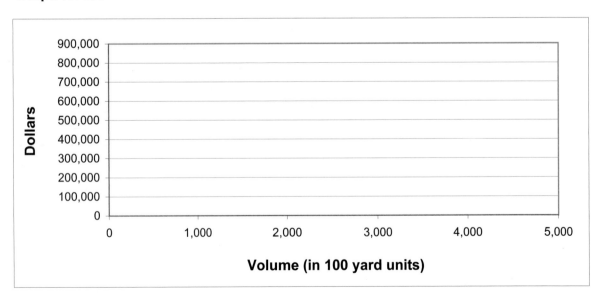

Graph for 2B

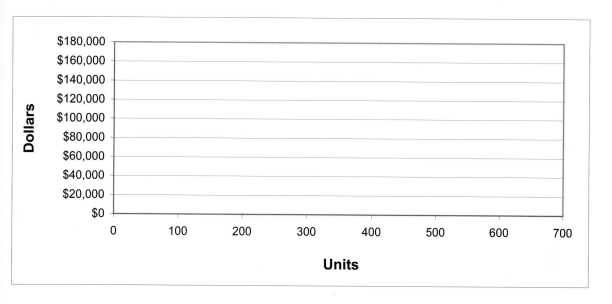

Part 3

_____

Contribution Margin Income Statement (at Break-Even)
Product_____

_____

_____

_____

_____

_____

_____

_____

Parts 1 and 2

Graph for 3A

Graph for 3B

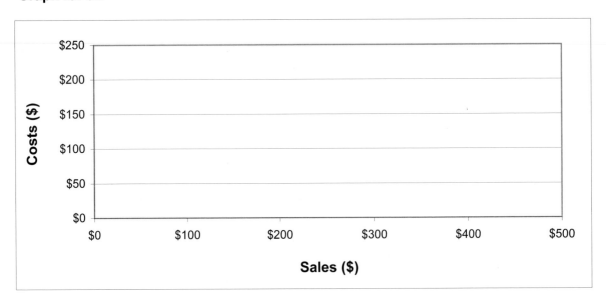

Variable costs per sales dollar:

_____

_____

Fixed costs:

_____

_____

_____

_____

Part 3

	Prediction	Prediction
Sales (given)	$	$
Fixed costs (from part 2)		
Variable costs (from part 2)		
Total costs		

Part 1

Year 20___ break-even in dollar sales: _____

_____

_____

_____

_____

_____

_____

_____

_____

_____

Part 2

Year 20___ break-even in dollar sales: _____

_____

_____

_____

_____

_____

_____

_____

_____

_____

_____

_____

Part 3

_____

_____

Forecasted Contribution Margin Income Statement
For Year Ended December 31, 20___

_____

_____

_____

_____

_____

_____

_____

Part 4

Required sales in dollars:

_____
_____
_____
_____
_____
_____
_____
_____
_____

Required sales in units:

_____
_____
_____
_____
_____
_____
_____
_____
_____
_____
_____

Part 5

_____
_____

Forecasted Contribution Margin Income Statement
For Year Ended December 31, 20_____

_____
_____
_____
_____
_____
_____
_____
_____
_____

Part 1

Break-even in dollar sales: _____

____Product_____: _____

_____

_____

_____

_____

_____

_____

_____

____Product_____: _____

_____

_____

_____

_____

_____

_____

_____

Part 2

_____COMPANY		
Forecasted Contribution Margin Income Statement		
	Product _____	*Product _____*

Part 3

_____COMPANY		
Forecasted Contribution Margin Income Statement		
	Product _____	*Product _____*

Part 4

Identification and Explanation of Greatest Change in Product Income (Loss) _____

_____

_____

_____

_____

_____

_____

_____

Part 5

Description of Potential Factors Yielding Different Product Cost Structures _____

_____

_____

_____

_____

_____

_____

_____

Part 1

(a) Plan 1's (or Existing Strategy for 6B) break-even in dollar sales: _____

_____
_____
_____
_____
_____
_____
_____
_____
_____

(b) Plan 2's (or New Strategy for 6B) break-even in dollar sales: _____

_____
_____
_____
_____
_____
_____
_____
_____
_____
_____

Part 2

_____COMPANY		
Forecasted Contribution Margin Income Statement		
	Plan 1 (or Existing Strategy)	*Plan 2 (or New Strategy)*

Chapter 21   Problem 21-7A or 21-7B   *Name* _____

Part 1

Break-even analysis assuming use of <u>same</u> materials: _____
   Step 1: Compute break-even in composite units

_____
_____
_____
_____
_____
_____
_____
_____
_____
_____
_____
_____
_____
_____

   Step 2: Compute break-even in individual product units sales

_____
_____
_____
_____
_____
_____
_____
_____

   Step 3: Compute break-even in individual product dollar sales

_____
_____
_____
_____
_____
_____
_____

Part 2

Break-even analysis assuming use of <u>new</u> materials:

   Step 1: Compute break-even in composite units

_____
_____
_____
_____
_____
_____
_____
_____
_____
_____
_____
_____
_____

   Step 2: Compute break-even in individual product unit sales

_____
_____
_____
_____
_____
_____
_____
_____

   Step 3: Compute break-even in individual product dollar sales

_____
_____
_____
_____
_____
_____
_____

Part 3

Management Insight for Long-Term Planning

_____
_____
_____
_____

1. Selling price per composite unit

_____

_____

_____

_____

_____

2. Variable costs per composite unit

_____

_____

_____

_____

_____

3. Break-even point in composite units

_____

_____

_____

_____

_____

4. Unit sales of desk units and chairs at break-even point

_____

_____

_____

_____

_____

(1) Identification of Costs _____

_____

_____

_____

_____

_____

_____

_____

_____

_____

_____

(2) _____

_____

_____

_____

_____

_____

_____

_____

_____

_____

_____

(3) _____

_____

_____

_____

_____

_____

_____

_____

_____

_____

_____

Name _____

(1)

	Polaris	Arctic Cat

(2) _____

_____

_____

_____

_____

_____

_____

_____

_____

_____

_____

_____

MEMORANDUM

To: "Mechanics" and "Owners"

From:

Re: Analysis of labor costs from survey data

Date:

REPORT ON REVENUE & COST ASSUMPTIONS

Revenue Assumptions:

_____
_____
_____
_____
_____
_____
_____
_____
_____
_____
_____
_____

Cost Assumptions:

_____
_____
_____
_____
_____
_____
_____
_____
_____
_____
_____
_____

Information and Resources Available for Entrepreneurs _____

_____

_____

_____

_____

_____

_____

_____

_____

_____

_____

_____

_____

_____

_____

_____

_____

_____

_____

_____

_____

_____

_____

_____

_____

Questions for Completion of CVP Analysis

For School Administration:

_____
_____
_____
_____
_____
_____
_____
_____
_____
_____
_____
_____
_____
_____
_____
_____

For Business Owner:

_____
_____
_____
_____
_____
_____
_____
_____
_____
_____
_____
_____
_____
_____
_____
_____
_____

(1) _____

_____

_____

_____

_____

_____

_____

_____

_____

_____

(2) _____

_____

_____

_____

_____

_____

_____

_____

_____

(3) _____

_____

_____

_____

_____

_____

_____

_____

_____

_____

(1) Potential Framework for Analysis

Product	Estimated Selling Price per unit	Estimated CM ratio	Estimated CM per unit	Estimated Sales Mix	Estimated CM for each component in composite unit

Total contribution margin (CM) per composite unit...................

Estimated fixed costs per year: $_____

Break-even point in composite unit sales: $_____/$CM per composite unit =

Unit sales of individual products per year required to break-even: _____

(2) Report on Results of Analysis from Part 1 (including break-even analysis)

_____
_____
_____
_____
_____
_____
_____
_____
_____
_____
_____
_____
_____
_____
_____
_____
_____
_____
_____
_____
_____
_____
_____
_____
_____
_____
_____
_____
_____
_____
_____

(1) Single or Multi-Product CVP Analysis

_____
_____
_____
_____
_____
_____

(2) Products Impact for Cost Analysis

_____
_____
_____
_____
_____
_____
_____
_____
_____
_____

Necessary Component of Master Budget: _____

_____

Quick Study 22-2

(1) _____

(2) _____

(3) _____

_____

Quick Study 22-3

_____ Company
Computation of Budgeted Cost of Purchases
For Month Ended July 31

_____

_____

_____

_____

_____

_____

_____

Quick Study 22-4

(1) Comparative Analysis of Budgeting Approaches: _____

_____

_____

(2) Examples of Bottom-Up Budgeting: _____

_____

_____

_____

Computation of Budgeted Accounts Receivable Balance:

_____
_____
_____
_____
_____
_____
_____
_____

Quick Study 22-6

_____ Company
Cash Budget
For Month Ended March 31

_____
_____
_____
_____
_____
_____
_____
_____
_____
_____
_____

Quick Study 22-7

_____
_____
_____
_____
_____

(2) Explanation of Differences between Activity-Based and Traditional Budgeting

_____
_____
_____

_____ Company
Production Budget
For Month Ended November 30

_____
_____
_____
_____
_____
_____
_____
_____
_____

Quick Study 22-9[A]

_____ Company
Factory Overhead Budget
For Month Ended November 30

_____
_____
_____
_____
_____
_____
_____
_____
_____
_____

Quick Study 22-10

_____
Sales Budget
For Month Ended June 30

_____
_____
_____
_____
_____
_____
_____
_____
_____
_____

_____
Selling Expense Budget
For Month Ended June 30

Quick Study 22-12

_____
Budgeted Cash Receipts
For Month Ended June 30

Quick Study 22-13

Cash Receipts Budget
For Month Ended September 30

Quick Study 22-15

Budgeted Cash Receipts
For Month Ended November 30

Quick Study 22-16

Cash Disbursements for Merchandise (Budgeted)
For Month Ended September 30

Cash Disbursements for Merchandise (Budgeted)			
For January, February, and March			
	January	February	March

Quick Study 22-18

Purchases Budget
For Month Ended April 30

Quick Study 22-19

Merchandise Purchases Budget			
For April, May, and June			
	April	May	June

_____
Production Budget
For Month Ended May 31

Quick Study 22-21

_____
Direct Materials Budget
For Month Ended January 31

Quick Study 22-22

_____
Direct Labor Budget
For Month Ended July 31

	Sales Budget		
	For January, February, and March		
	Budgeted Unit Sales	Budgeted Unit Price	Budgeted Total Sales

Quick Study 22-24

	Cash Receipts Budget		
	For January, February, and March		
	January	February	March

Quick Study 22-25

	Selling Expense Budget		
	For January, February, and March		
	January	February	March

_____		
Cash Budget		
For Month Ended February 28		

_____
_____
_____
_____
_____
_____
_____
_____
_____

Quick Study 22-27

(1) _____
_____
_____

(2) _____
_____
_____
_____

_____ Company			
Cash Budget			
For January, February, and March			
	January	February	March

_____ Company			
Merchandise Purchases Budget			
For July, August and September			
	July	August	September

Supporting calculations:

_____

_____

_____

_____

_____

_____

_____

_____

_____

_____

_____

_____

_____

_____

_____

_____

_____

_____

(2) Ratio of Ending Inventory to Next Month's Sales

_____

_____

(3) Units Budgeted for Sale in October

_____

_____

_____ Company
Cash Budget
For Month Ended July 31

Supporting calculations:

_____ Company
Budgeted Income Statement
For Month Ended July 31

Supporting calculations:

_____ Company
Budgeted Balance Sheet
July 31

Merchandise purchases budgets

	August	September	October

Cash payments for purchases (on accounts) in October

	Dollars	Percent	Paid

(1) Budgeted merchandise purchases:

	June	July	August

(2) Budgeted cost of goods sold:

	June	July	August

Exercise 22-7

(1) Budgeted merchandise purchases:

	July	August	September	October

Supporting calculations:

_____
_____
_____
_____
_____
_____
_____
_____
_____
_____

(2) Budgeted payments on accounts payable in September:

	Purchases	*Percent Paid*	*Dollars Paid*

Budgeted payments on accounts payable in October:

	Purchases	*Percent Paid*	*Dollars Paid*

(3) Budgeted balance of accounts payable at the end of September:

	Purchases	*Percent Unpaid*	*Dollars Unpaid*

Budgeted balance of accounts payable at the end of October:

	Purchases	*Percent Unpaid*	*Dollars Unpaid*

	Company	
	Production Budget	
	For Second and Third Quarters	
	Second Quarter	**Third Quarter**

Exercise 22-9[A]

	Company	
	Direct Materials Budget	
	For Second Quarter	

_____ Company
Direct Labor Budget
For Second Quarter

_____ Company		
Budgeted Cash Disbursements		
For August and September		
	August	**September**

Exercise 22-12

_____ Company			
Cash Receipts Budget			
For April, May, and June			
	April	**May**	**June**

_____ Company			
Cash Budget			
For July, August, and September			
	July	August	September

Exercise 22-14

_____ Company			
Cash Budget			
For October, November, and December			
	October	November	December

| | Cash Budget | | |
| | For April, May, and June | | |
	April	May	June

| | Cash Budget | | |
| | For April, May, and June | | |
	April	May	June

Cash Receipts Budget For July, August, and September			
	July	August	September

Cash Budget For July, August, and September			
	July	August	September

_____ Company
Budgeted Balance Sheet
March 31

	Budgeted Income Statement	
	For Quarter Ended March 31	

_____

Supporting calculations:

_____

_____ Company Direct Labor Budget For July, August, and September	July	August	September

Exercise 22-20

_____ Company Production Budget For April, May, and June	April	May	June

Direct Materials Budget			
For April, May, and June			
	April	May	June

(1) _____

(2) _____

(3) _____

(4) _____

(5) _____

(6) _____

(7) _____

(8) _____

(9) _____

Exercise 22-23

_____

_____

_____

_____

_____

_____

Exercise 22-24

_____ Company Activity-Based Budget For Year Ended December 31, 20____	Budgeted Hours	Budgeted Price/Hour	Budgeted Cost

_____
Direct Materials Budget
For Second Quarter

Part 1

Direct Materials Budget
For Second Quarter

Part 2

Factory Overhead Budget
For Second Quarter

_____ Company Direct Materials Budget For April, May, and June	April	May	June

Name _____

Part 1

	April	May	June
_____ Company			
Direct Labor Budget			
For April, May, and June			

Part 2

	April	May	June
_____ Company			
Factory Overhead Budget			
For April, May, and June			

Part 1

_____ Merchandise Purchases Budgets (in Units) For Months of _____	Month of _____	Month of _____	Month of _____
Product: _____			
Product: _____			
Product: _____			

Part 2

Identification and Explanation of Factors Yielding Fewer Purchases

_____
_____
_____
_____
_____
_____
_____
_____
_____
_____
_____
_____
_____
_____
_____
_____
_____
_____
_____
_____
_____

	Cash Budgets For Months of _____		
	Month of _____	**Month of** _____	**Month of** _____

Supporting computations: _____

_____

_____

_____

_____

_____

_____

_____

_____

_____

_____

_____

_____

_____

_____

_____

_____

Part 1

Cash collections of credit sales (accounts receivable)

From sales in month of:	Total	% Collected	Month of _____	Month of _____

Part 2

Budgeted ending inventories (in units)

	Month of _____	Month of _____	Month of _____	Month of _____

Part 3

_____Company Merchandise Purchases Budgets For Months of_____	Month of _____	Month of _____	Month of _____

Part 4

Cash payments on product purchases

From purchases in month of:	*Total*	*% Paid*	Month of _____	Month of _____

Part 5

Cash Budgets For Months of_____	Month of _____	Month of _____

Part 6

Benefits to Management from Accurate Cash Budget Numbers _____

_____
_____
_____
_____
_____
_____
_____
_____
_____
_____
_____
_____

Part 1

	Budgeted Income Statements For Months of _____		
	Month of _____	Month of _____	Month of _____

Part 2: Recommendation on Implementation of Proposed Changes

_____
_____
_____
_____
_____
_____
_____
_____
_____
_____
_____
_____

Part 1

Sales Budgets For Months of _____			
Month	**Budgeted Units**	**Budgeted Unit Price**	**Budgeted Total Dollars**

Part 2

Merchandise Purchases Budgets For Months of _____			
	Month of _____	**Month of** _____	**Month of** _____	**Total**

Part 3

Selling Expense Budgets For Months of _____			
	Month of _____	**Month of** _____	**Month of** _____	**Total**

Part 4

	General and Administrative Expense Budgets For Months of_____			
	Month of _____	Month of _____	Month of _____	Total

Supporting calculations:

Part 5

	Capital Expenditures Budgets For Months of_____		
	Month of _____	Month of _____	Month of _____

Part 6

	Cash Budgets For Months of _____		
	Month of _____	Month of _____	Month of _____

Part 7

_____	
Budgeted Income Statement	
For Three Months Ended_____	

Budgeted Balance Sheet

Part 1

Production Budget (in units)
For _____ Quarter

_____
_____
_____
_____
_____
_____
_____
_____

Part 2

Direct Materials Budget (in lbs., except where noted)
For _____ Quarter

_____
_____
_____
_____
_____
_____
_____
_____
_____
_____
_____

Direct Labor Budget	
For Third Quarter	

Factory Overhead Budget	
For Third Quarter	

Part 1

| | Sales Budgets | | |
| Month | For Months of_____ | | |
	Budgeted Units	Budgeted Unit Price	Budgeted Total Dollars

Part 2

| | Production Budgets | | | |
| | For Months of_____ | | | |
	Month of _____	Month of _____	Month of _____	Total

Part 3

| | Raw Mateials Budgets | | | |
| | For Months of_____ | | | |
	Month of _____	Month of _____	Month of _____	Total

Part 4

	Direct Labor Budgets For Months of _____			
	Month of _____	Month of _____	Month of _____	Total

Part 5

	Factory Overhead Budgets For Months of _____			
	Month of _____	Month of _____	Month of _____	Total

Part 6

	Selling Expense Budgets For Months of _____			
	Month of _____	Month of _____	Month of _____	Total

Part 7

	General and Administrative Expense Budgets **For Months of** _____			
	Month of _____	**Month of** _____	**Month of** _____	**Total**

Part 8

	Cash Budgets For Months of_____		
	Month of _____	Month of _____	Month of _____

Part 9

Budgeted Income Statement
For Three Months Ended_____

Budgeted Balance Sheet

_____

_____

_____

_____

_____

_____

_____

_____

_____

_____

_____

_____

_____

_____

_____

_____

_____

_____

_____

_____

_____

_____

_____

_____

_____

_____

Budgeted Statement of Retained Earnings
For Three Months Ended_____

Part 1

SUCCESS SYSTEMS Budgeted Income Statements For Months of April, May and June			
	April	May	June

Part 2: Recommendation on Implementation of Proposed Changes _____

_____
_____
_____
_____
_____
_____
_____
_____
_____
_____
_____
_____

Part 1

_____
_____
_____
_____
_____
_____
_____
_____
_____
_____
_____
_____
_____

Part 2

(a) _____
_____
_____
_____

(b) _____
_____
_____
_____

Part 3

FastForward: _____
_____
_____
_____
_____
_____
_____
_____
_____

Name _____

Part 1

Computation of inventory reduction under new distribution system

Amount of ending inventory required at the 30% rule.... $ _____

Amount of ending inventory required at the 10% rule....   _____

Difference (inventory reduction)................................ $ _____

Implication of Distribution System for Inventory Level: _____

_____

_____

_____

_____

Part 2

Explanation and Justification of JIT Inventory System _____

_____

_____

_____

_____

_____

_____

_____

_____

_____

_____

_____

_____

_____

_____

_____

_____

Report on "Use It or Lose It" Budgeting

MEMORANDUM

TO: _____

FROM: _____

DATE: _____

SUBJECT: Concerns with sales staff input for the sales budget

---

Part 1

Benefits of Using e-Budgets _____

_____
_____
_____
_____
_____
_____
_____
_____
_____
_____
_____
_____
_____
_____

Part 2

Concerns with the Concept and Application of e-Budgets _____

_____
_____
_____
_____
_____
_____
_____
_____
_____
_____
_____
_____
_____
_____
_____
_____

College Costs Budget

Part 1

Business Plan Elements _____

_____
_____
_____
_____
_____
_____
_____

Part 2

Benefits of Budgeting _____

_____
_____
_____
_____
_____
_____
_____

Hitting the Road—BTN 22-8

Part 1

Identification of External Factors When Setting Budgets _____

_____
_____
_____
_____
_____

Part 2

Identification of Potential Factors Explaining Price Differences _____

_____
_____
_____
_____

Part 1

Importance of Administrative Expense Budget in Its Master Budgeting Process _____

_____
_____
_____
_____
_____
_____
_____
_____
_____

Part 2

Identification of Administrative Expenses _____

_____
_____
_____
_____
_____

Part 3

Identification and Explanation of Person Responsible for Administrative Expense Budget ____

_____
_____
_____
_____
_____
_____

_____ Company		
Flexible Budget Performance Report		
For Month Ended May 31		
Flexible Budget	*Actual Results*	*Variances*

Quick Study 23-2

Quick Study 23-3

Cost Variance

Quick Study 23-4

(1) Description of Management by Exception Concept

(2) Explanation of How Standard Costs Aid Management by Exception

Actual Total Direct Materials Cost _____

_____
_____
_____
_____
_____
_____
_____

Quick Study 23-6

Actual Total Direct Labor Cost _____

_____
_____
_____
_____
_____
_____

Quick Study 23-7

Actual Pounds of Materials Used _____

_____
_____
_____
_____
_____
_____
_____
_____
_____
_____
_____

Quick Study 23-8

Actual Total Overhead Cost _____

_____
_____
_____
_____
_____
_____
_____

GENERAL JOURNAL

Date	Account Titles and Explanation	PR	Debit	Credit

Quick Study 23-10^A

Total Variable Overhead Cost Variance: _____

_____

_____

_____

_____

_____

Quick Study 23-11^A

Variable Overhead Spending and Efficiency Variances: _____

_____

_____

_____

_____

_____

_____

_____

_____

_____

_____

Sales	Actual	Flexible Budget	Fixed Budget
Units			
Price per unit			
Total dollars			

Quick Study 23-13
Total Budgeted Costs (Flexible Budget)

_____
_____
_____
_____

Quick Study 23-14

_____
_____
_____
_____
_____
_____
_____
_____
_____

_____ Company Flexible Budget Performance Report For Month Ended December 31			
	Flexible *Budget*	*Actual* *Results*	*Variances*

Quick Study 23-16

Direct Materials Price Variance
_____
_____
_____
_____

Direct Materials Quantity Variance
_____
_____
_____
_____

Quick Study 23-17

Direct Labor Rate Variance
_____
_____
_____
_____

Direct Labor Efficiency Variance
_____
_____
_____
_____

_____
_____
_____
_____
_____
_____
_____

Quick Study 23-19

_____
_____
_____
_____
_____
_____
_____

Quick Study 23-20

_____
_____
_____
_____
_____
_____

Quick Study 23-21

Sales	Actual	Flexible Budget	Fixed Budget
Units			
Price per unit			
Total dollars			

Item	Cost behavior
a. Bike frames	
b. Screws for assembly	
c. Repair expense for tools	
d. Direct labor	
e. Tires	
f. Gas used for heating	
g. Incoming shipping expenses	
h. Taxes on property	
i. Office supplies	
j. Depreciation on tools	
k. Management salaries	

_____ Company				
Flexible Budgets				
For Quarter Ended March 31, 20___				
Flexible Budget		*Flexible*	*Flexible*	*Flexible*
Variable	*Total*	*Budget for*	*Budget for*	*Budget for*
Amount	*Fixed*	*Unit Sales*	*Unit Sales*	*Unit Sales*
per Unit	*Cost*	*of* _____	*of* _____	*of* _____

_____ Company Flexible Budget Performance Report For Month Ended June 30	Flexible Budget	Actual Results	Variances

Supporting calculations:

_____

_____

_____

_____

_____

_____

_____

_____

_____

_____

_____

_____

_____

_____

_____

_____ Company Flexible Budget Performance Report For Month Ended July 31	Flexible Budget	Actual Results	Variances

Supporting calculations:

_____

_____

_____

_____

_____

_____

_____

_____

_____

_____

_____

_____

_____

_____

_____

_____

Part 1

October variances:

_____

_____
_____
_____
_____
_____
_____
_____
_____
_____
_____
_____
_____
_____
_____
_____
_____
_____
_____
_____

November variances:

_____

_____
_____
_____
_____
_____
_____
_____
_____
_____
_____
_____
_____
_____
_____
_____
_____
_____
_____
_____

Interpretation of October Direct labor Variances _____

_____
_____
_____
_____
_____
_____
_____
_____

Exercise 23-6
Part 1
Predetermined Overhead Rate Computations: _____

_____
_____
_____
_____
_____
_____
_____

Part 2
Variable Overhead Cost Variance: _____

_____
_____
_____
_____
_____

Fixed Overhead Cost Variance: _____

_____
_____
_____
_____

Preliminary Computations for Predetermined overhead rates (see Exercise 23-6):

_____
_____
_____
_____
_____
_____
_____
_____

Part 1

Variable overhead spending and efficiency variances:
    Computations:

_____
_____
_____
_____
_____
_____
_____
_____
_____
_____

    Interpretation:

_____
_____
_____
_____
_____
_____
_____
_____

Part 2

Fixed overhead spending and volume variances
    Computations:

_____

_____

_____

_____

_____

_____

_____

_____

_____

_____

_____

_____

_____

_____

_____

_____

_____

_____

_____

_____

    Interpretation:

_____

_____

_____

_____

_____

_____

_____

_____

Part 3

Controllable Variance:

_____
_____
_____
_____
_____
_____
_____

Interpretation:

_____
_____
_____
_____
_____

Part 1

Computation of Direct Materials Variances:

_____
_____
_____
_____
_____
_____
_____
_____
_____
_____
_____
_____
_____
_____
_____
_____
_____
_____
_____
_____
_____
_____
_____
_____
_____
_____
_____
_____
_____
_____
_____
_____

Part 2

Interpretation of Direct Materials Variances:

_____
_____
_____
_____

Chapter 23   Exercise 23-9^A *Name* _____

Part 1

GENERAL JOURNAL

Date	Account Titles and Explanation	PR	Debit	Credit

Part 2

GENERAL JOURNAL

Date	Account Titles and Explanation	PR	Debit	Credit

Part 3

Identification of Variance Investigated if Applying Management by Exception _____

_____

_____

_____

_____

_____

_____

Part 1

Total Overhead Planned at ____% Level: _____

_____

_____

_____

_____

_____

Part 2

Total Overhead Variance: _____

_____

_____

_____

_____

_____

Preliminary Computations of Total Overhead Variances: _____

_____
_____
_____
_____
_____
_____
_____
_____
_____
_____
_____
_____
_____

Part 1

Computation of Overhead Volume Variance _____

_____
_____
_____
_____
_____
_____
_____
_____
_____
_____
_____
_____
_____
_____
_____
_____
_____
_____
_____
_____
_____
_____
_____

Part 2

Computation of Overhead Controllable Variance _____

_____

_____

_____

_____

_____

_____

_____

_____

_____

_____

_____

_____

_____

_____

_____

_____

_____

_____

_____

_____

_____

(1) Computation of Sales Price and Sales Volume Variances

_____
_____
_____
_____
_____
_____
_____
_____
_____
_____
_____
_____
_____
_____
_____
_____
_____
_____
_____
_____
_____
_____
_____

(2) Interpretation of Variances from Part 1

_____
_____
_____
_____
_____
_____

(a) _____
(b) _____
(c) _____
(d) _____
(e) _____

Exercise 23-14

(1) _____
(2) _____
(3) _____
(4) _____
(5) _____
(6) _____
(7) _____
(8) _____
(9) _____
(10) _____

Exercise 23-15

_____
_____
_____
_____
_____
_____

Part 1

Direct Materials Price Variance _____

_____

_____

_____

_____

Direct Materials Quantity Variance _____

_____

_____

_____

_____

Part 2

Direct Labor Rate Variance _____

_____

_____

_____

Direct Labor Efficiency Variance _____

_____

_____

_____

_____

Part 1

Direct Materials Cost Variances

_____

_____
_____
_____
_____
_____
_____
_____
_____
_____
_____
_____
_____
_____
_____
_____
_____
_____
_____
_____
_____
_____
_____
_____
_____
_____
_____
_____
_____
_____
_____
_____
_____

Part 2

Direct Labor Cost Variances

_____
_____
_____
_____
_____
_____
_____
_____
_____
_____
_____
_____
_____
_____
_____
_____
_____
_____
_____
_____
_____
_____
_____
_____
_____

Part 3

Overhead Cost Variance:

_____
_____
_____
_____
_____
_____
_____
_____
_____

(a) Variable Overhead Spending and Efficiency Variances _____

_____
_____
_____
_____
_____
_____
_____
_____
_____
_____
_____
_____
_____
_____
_____
_____
_____
_____
_____
_____
_____
_____
_____
_____
_____
_____
_____
_____
_____
_____
_____
_____
_____
_____
_____
_____
_____
_____
_____
_____
_____
_____

(b) Fixed Overhead Spending and Volume Variances

(c) Total Overhead Controllable Variance

Part 1

Variable or Fixed Classification	*Amount*

_____Company
Flexible Budgets
For Year Ended December 31, _____

	Flexible Budget		*Flexible*	*Flexible*
	Variable	*Total*	*Budget for*	*Budget for*
	Amount	*Fixed*	*Unit Sales*	*Unit Sales*
	per Unit	*Cost*	*of* _____	*of* _____
_____				
_____				
_____				
_____				
_____				
_____				
_____				
_____				
_____				
_____				
_____				
_____				
_____				
_____				
_____				
_____				
_____				
_____				
_____				
_____				
_____				
_____				

Part 3
Operating income increase for a _____ to _____ unit sales increase:

_____

_____

_____

_____

_____

_____

_____

_____

Part 4

Operating income (loss) at _____ units:

_____
_____
_____
_____
_____
_____
_____
_____
_____
_____

Problem 23-4A or 23-4B

Part 1

_____Company Flexible Budget Performance Report For Year Ended December 31, _____		
Flexible *Budget*	*Actual* *Results*	*Variances*

Part 2

(a) Analysis of sales variance

	Total	*Per Unit*

Interpretation:

_____

_____

_____

_____

(b) Analysis of direct materials variance

	Total	*Per Unit*

Interpretation:

_____

_____

_____

_____

Part 1

Variable or Fixed Classification	Amount
Variable costs (per unit):	
Fixed costs (per month):	

Part 2

_____Company Flexible Overhead Budgets For Month Ended _____				
Flexible Budget		Flexible	Flexible	Flexible
Variable	Total	Budget for	Budget for	Budget for
Amount	Fixed	Unit Sales	Unit Sales	Unit Sales
per Unit	Cost	of _____	of _____	of _____

Part 3

Direct Materials Cost Variances

_____
_____
_____
_____
_____
_____
_____
_____
_____
_____
_____
_____
_____
_____
_____
_____
_____
_____
_____
_____
_____
_____
_____
_____
_____
_____
_____
_____
_____
_____
_____
_____

Part 4

Direct Labor Cost Variances

Part 5

_____Company Overhead Variance Report For Month Ended _____			
Volume Variance			
	Flexible	**Actual**	
Controllable Variance	**Budget**	**Results**	**Variances**

Part 1

Direct Materials Cost Variances

_____
_____
_____
_____
_____
_____
_____
_____
_____
_____
_____
_____
_____
_____
_____
_____
_____
_____
_____
_____
_____
_____
_____
_____
_____
_____
_____
_____
_____
_____
_____
_____
_____
_____
_____
_____
_____
_____

Direct Labor Cost Variances

Part 3

(a) Variable Overhead Spending and Efficiency Variances

_____

_____
_____
_____
_____
_____
_____
_____
_____
_____
_____
_____
_____
_____
_____
_____
_____
_____
_____
_____
_____
_____
_____
_____
_____
_____
_____
_____
_____
_____
_____
_____
_____
_____
_____
_____
_____

(b) Fixed Overhead Spending and Volume Variances

_____
_____
_____
_____
_____
_____
_____
_____
_____
_____
_____
_____
_____
_____
_____
_____
_____
_____
_____
_____
_____
_____
_____
_____
_____
_____

(c) Total Overhead Controllable Variance

_____
_____
_____
_____
_____
_____
_____
_____
_____

Part 4

_____Company Overhead Variance Report For Month Ended _____			
Volume Variance			
Controllable Variance	**Flexible Budget**	**Actual Results**	**Variances**

Part 1

GENERAL JOURNAL

Date	Account Titles and Explanation	PR	Debit	Credit

Part 2

Identification of Areas and Actions when Applying Management by Exception

_____
_____
_____
_____
_____
_____
_____
_____
_____
_____
_____
_____
_____
_____

SUCCESS SYSTEMS			
Flexible Budget Performance Report			
For Quarter Ended June 30			
	Flexible Budget	Actual Results	Variances
Desk Sales............................			
Chair Sales...........................			
Variable expenses..................			
Contribution margin...............			
Fixed expenses......................			
Income from operations.........			

Supporting computations:

_____
_____
_____
_____
_____
_____
_____
_____
_____

Part 1

Identification of Foreign Currency Translation (FTC) Information

_____
_____
_____
_____

Part 2

_____
_____
_____
_____
_____
_____
_____
_____
_____
_____
_____
_____

Chapter 23   Comparative Analysis   *Name* _____
                 BTN 23-2

Part 1

	2 Years Prior	1 Year Prior	Current year	1 Year Ahead	2 Years Ahead
Polaris					
Arctic Cat					

Part 2

Explanation of Sales Predictions _____

_____

_____

_____

_____

Ethics Challenge—BTN 23-3

Specialty	Information Input and Explanation

<table>
<tr><td colspan="2" align="center">**MEMORANDUM**</td></tr>
</table>

MEMORANDUM	
TO:	_____
FROM:	_____
DATE:	_____
SUBJECT:	Explanation and Implications of Favorable and Unfavorable Variances

_____
_____
_____
_____
_____
_____
_____
_____
_____
_____
_____
_____
_____
_____
_____
_____
_____
_____
_____
_____
_____
_____
_____
_____
_____
_____
_____
_____
_____

Name _____

Part 1

Explanation of Benchmarking _____

_____
_____
_____
_____
_____
_____
_____
_____
_____
_____
_____
_____
_____
_____

Part 2

Relation between Standard Costing and Benchmarking _____

_____
_____
_____
_____
_____
_____
_____
_____
_____
_____
_____

Identification and Description of Time Elements Used for Competitive Advantage

_____

_____

_____

_____

_____

_____

_____

_____

_____

_____

_____

_____

_____

_____

_____

_____

_____

_____

_____

_____

_____

_____

_____

_____

_____

_____

_____

_____

_____

_____

MEMORANDUM

TO: _____
FROM: _____
DATE: _____
SUBJECT: Explanation of Standard Costing and Variance Comments

_____
_____
_____
_____
_____
_____
_____
_____
_____
_____
_____
_____
_____
_____
_____
_____
_____
_____
_____
_____
_____
_____
_____
_____
_____
_____
_____
_____
_____

(1) Observe and Record the Number and Application of Raw Materials to Pizza

_____
_____
_____
_____
_____

(2) Identify and Record Differences Across the Two Businesses in Part 1

_____
_____
_____
_____
_____
_____

(3) Estimate and Explain which Business is More Profitable

_____
_____
_____
_____
_____
_____

Global Decision—BTN 23-9

(1)

	One Year Prior	Current Year	One Year Ahead	Two Years Ahead
Sales				

(2) Estimation and Explanation of Sales Predictions

_____
_____
_____
_____
_____
_____

(1) _____   (5) _____
(2) _____   (6) _____
(3) _____   (7) _____
(4) _____

Quick Study 24-2

(1) _____
_____

(2) _____
_____

(3) _____
_____

(4) _____
_____
_____

Quick Study 24-3

1. _____
2. _____
3. _____
4. _____

Contribution to Overhead (dollars):	
Dept. A	
Dept. B	
Dept. C	
Contribution to Overhead (percent of sales):	
Dept. A	
Dept. B	
Dept. C	

Highest Contribution

Dollar	
Percent	

Quick Study 24-5

Center	Net Income	Average Assets	Return on Assets
Cameras & Camcorders	$ 4,500,000	$ 20,000,000	
Phones & Communications	1,500,000	12,500,000	
Computers & Accessories	800,000	10,000,000	

Center Performance Evaluation:

_____
_____
_____
_____

Quick Study 24-6

	Cameras & Camcorders	Phones & Communications	Computers & Accessories

Profit Margin:

_____

_____

Return on assets:

_____

_____

Investment Turnover:

_____

_____

Quick Study 24-8

INVESTMENT CENTER A
Return on assets:

_____

_____

Profit Margin:

_____

_____

Investment Turnover:

_____

_____

INVESTMENT CENTER B
Return on assets:

_____

_____

Profit Margin:

_____

_____

Investment Turnover:

_____

_____

1. _____	5. _____
2. _____	6 _____
3. _____	7. _____
4. _____	8. _____

Quick Study 24-10

_____

_____

_____

_____

Quick Study 24-11^{A}

Transfer Price Determination:

_____
_____
_____
_____
_____
_____

Range of Transfer Prices: _____

_____

_____

_____

_____

_____

_____

Quick Study 24-13^B

Joint Cost Assigned to Unit B Using the Value Basis of Allocation _____

_____

_____

_____

_____

_____

_____

_____

_____

_____

_____

_____

_____

_____

_____

Step 1: Allocate total rent expense between the floors.

	Amount Allocated	% of Total	Cost
First floor			
Second floor			
Totals			

Step 2: Allocate the floors' rent expense to the separate departments.

First Floor	Sq. Feet	% of Total	Cost
Paint Dept.			
Engine Dept.			
Totals			

Second Floor	Sq. Feet	% of Total	Cost
Window Dept.			
Electrical Dept.			
Accessory Dept.			
Totals			

Quick Study 24-15

Average invested assets: _____

_____

Return on assets: _____

_____

_____

Quick Study 24-16

a. _____

_____

_____

b. _____

_____

_____

(1) Allocation of Indirect Expenses to Operating Departments
Supervision:

	Employees	% of Total	Cost
Materials			
Personnel			
Manufacturing			
Packaging			
Totals			

Utilities:

	Square Feet	% of Total	Cost
Materials			
Personnel			
Manufacturing			
Packaging			
Totals			

Insurance:

	Asset Value	% of Total	Cost
Materials			
Personnel			
Manufacturing			
Packaging			
Totals			

(2) Total indirect expenses assigned to operating departments:

	Supervision	Utilities	Insurance	Totals
Materials				
Personnel				
Manufacturing				
Packaging				
Totals				

Definitely Included:

_____
_____
_____
_____
_____
_____

Definitely Excluded:

_____
_____
_____
_____
_____
_____

Neither Definitely Included nor Definitely Excluded:

_____
_____
_____
_____
_____
_____
_____

Part 1

Income Statement Showing Departmental Contribution to Overhead			
For Year Ended December 31, 20____			
	_____	_____	**Combined**

Part 2

_____
_____
_____
_____

	Allocation Base	Account Balance	Adver-tising	Admin-istrative	Shoes	Clothing
Department Expense Allocation Spreadsheet						
For Year Ended December 31, 20___						
				Allocation of Expenses to Departments		
Direct expenses						
Indirect utilities expense						
Total dept. expense						
Service dept. expenses:						
Advertising						
Administrative						
Total expenses allocated to operating depts.						

Supplemental expense allocation calculations:

Utilities expense:

	Square Feet	% of Total	Cost
Advertising			
Administrative			
Shoes			
Clothing			
Total			

Advertising expense:

	Ads Placed	% of Total	Cost
Shoes			
Clothing			
Total			

Administrative expense:

	Sales	% of Total	Cost
Shoes			
Clothing			
Total			

	Allocation Base	Expense Account Balance	Allocation of Expenses to Departments				
_____ BOOKSTORE **Departmental Expense Allocation Spreadsheet** **For Period Ended_____**			Adver-tising Dept.	Purchas-ing Dept.	Books Dept.	Magazine Dept.	News-paper Dept.
Total dept. expenses.........							
Service dept. expenses:							
Advertising........	Sales						
Purchasing......	Purchase Orders						
Total expenses allocated to operating depts...............							

Allocations of service department costs to operating departments

Advertising: _____

	Sales	% of Total	Cost
Books Dept.			
Magazines Dept.			
Newspapers Dept.			
Totals			

Purchasing: _____

	Purchase Orders	% of Total	Cost
Books Dept.			
Magazines Dept.			
Newspapers Dept.			
Totals			

Allocation of annual wages between two departments

	*Hours Worked**	*% of Total*	*Cost*
Jewelry Dept.			
Hosiery Dept.			
Totals			

* Computation of hours worked in the two selling departments:
  Jewelry department:
        Selling……………………………
        Arranging and stocking………
  Hosiery department:
        Selling……………………………
        Arranging and stocking………
  Total hours…………………………

(1)

Location	Net Income	Average Assets	Return on Assets
Location A			
Location B			

(2)

MEMORANDUM

TO:

FROM:

DATE:

SUBJECT: Investment analysis and recommendation

(1)

Investment Center	Net Income	Average Assets	Return on Assets
Electronics			
Sporting Goods			

Comments: _____

_____

(2)

Investment Center	Electronics	Sporting Goods
Net Income		
Target Net Income		
Residual Income		

Comments: _____

_____

(3) _____

_____

Exercise 24-9

Investment Center	Net Income	Sales	Profit Margin
Electronics			
Sporting Goods			

Investment Center	Sales	Average Assets	Investment Turnover
Electronics			
Sporting Goods			

Comments: _____

_____

_____

_____

Name _____

1. _____   8. _____
2. _____   9. _____
3. _____   10. _____
4. _____   11. _____
5. _____   12. _____
6. _____   13. _____
7. _____   14. _____

Exercise 24-11[A]

(1) _____

_____

_____

_____

_____

_____

(2) _____

_____

_____

_____

_____

_____

(3) _____

_____

_____

_____

_____

_____

_____

_____

Preliminary calculations

Land Cost.......................

Improvements.................

Total cost of lots.............

Lots	Quantity	Price	Total
Canyon			
Hilltop			
Total Market value			

Allocated cost--value basis of allocation: _____

	Market Value	% of Total	Allocated Cost	Average Lot Cost
Canyon section				
Hilltop section				
Totals				

Preliminary calculations

Parts	Quantity	Price	Total
Lobster Tails			
Lobster Flakes			
Total market value			

_____

_____

_____

Allocated cost (value basis allocation): _____

Parts	Market Value	% of Total	Allocated Cost	Cost per lb.
Lobster Tails				
Lobster Flakes				
Total				

(1) Cost of goods sold

Parts	Quantity	Cost	Total
Lobster Tails			
Lobster Flakes			
Total cost of goods sold			

(2) Cost of ending inventory

Parts	Quantity	Cost	Total
Lobster Tails			
Lobster Flakes			
Total inventory cost			

(1)

Investment Center	Net Income	Sales	Profit Margin
Professional products			
Consumer products			
Luxury products			
Active Cosmetics			

(2)

Investment Center	Net Income	Average Assets	Investment Turnover
Professional products			
Consumer products			
Luxury products			
Active Cosmetics			

Part 1

Average occupancy cost = _____

These costs are assigned to departments as follows:

Department	Square Footage	Rate	Total
_____ Dept.			
_____ Dept. (for 1A)			

Part 2

VALUE-BASED costs are allocated to departments in two steps:

(i) Compute market value for each floor space.

Floor	Square Footage	Value per Sq. Ft.	Total
_____floor			
_____floor			
Basement floor (for 1B)			
Total market value			

(ii) Allocate $_____ to each floor based on its percent of market value.

	Market Value	% of Total	Allocated Cost	Cost per Sq. Ft.
_____floor				
_____floor				
Basement floor (for 1B)				
Totals				

USAGE-BASED costs allocation rate = _____

(i) Compute total allocation rates for the floors

Floor	Value	Usage	Total
_____floor			
_____floor			
Basement floor (for 1B)			

(ii) Rates are applied to allocate occupancy costs to department(s).

Department	Square Footage	Rate	Total
_____ Depart.			
_____ Depart. (for 1A)			

Part 3

Preferred Allocation Method _____

_____

_____

_____

_____

_____

_____

_____

_____				

Forecasted Departmental Income Statements
For Year Ended December 31, 20____

				Combined

<u>**Supporting computations:**</u>

_____
_____
_____
_____
_____
_____
_____
_____
_____
_____
_____
_____
_____
_____
_____
_____
_____
_____
_____
_____
_____
_____
_____
_____
_____
_____
_____
_____
_____
_____
_____
_____
_____
_____
_____
_____
_____
_____
_____
_____
_____
_____

(a)

RESPONSIBILITY ACCOUNTING PERFORMANCE REPORT			
Manager, _____ Department			
			For the _____
	Budgeted Amount	*Actual Amount*	*Over (Under) Budget*
CONTROLLABLE COSTS			
Raw materials			
Employee wages			
Supplies used			
Depreciation--Equipment			
Totals			

(b)

RESPONSIBILITY ACCOUNTING PERFORMANCE REPORT			
Manager, _____ Department			
			For the _____
	Budgeted Amount	*Actual Amount*	*Over (Under) Budget*
CONTROLLABLE COSTS			
Raw materials			
Employee wages			
Supplies used			
Depreciation--Equipment			
Totals			

(c)

RESPONSIBILITY ACCOUNTING PERFORMANCE REPORT			
Manager, _____ Plant			
			For the _____
	Budgeted Amount	*Actual Amount*	*Over (Under) Budget*
CONTROLLABLE COSTS			
Dept. manager salaries			
Utilities			
Building rent			
Other office salaries			
Other office costs			
_____ department			
_____ department			
Totals			

Part 2

Comparative Analysis of Manager Performance _____

_____

_____

_____

_____

_____

_____

_____

Problem 24-4A[B] or 24-4B[B]

Part 1

Allocation of joint costs on the basis of sales value

Cost Activity: _____

Grade	Sales Value	Percent of Total	Allocated Cost
No. 1			
No. 2			
No. 3			
Total			

Cost Activity: _____

Grade	Sales Value	Percent of Total	Allocated Cost
No. 1			
No. 2			
No. 3			
Total			

Cost Activity: _____

Grade	Sales Value	Percent of Total	Allocated Cost
No. 1			
No. 2			
No. 3			
Total			

Part 2

	Income Statement			
	For Year Ended December 31, 20___			
	No. 1	No. 2	No. 3	Combined

Part 3

Analysis of Joint Cost _____

_____

_____

_____

_____

_____

_____

_____

_____

_____

Part 1

_____
_____
_____
_____
_____
_____
_____
_____

Part 2

_____
_____
_____
_____
_____

Part 3

_____
_____
_____
_____
_____
_____
_____
_____

Part 1

_____
_____
_____
_____
_____
_____
_____
_____
_____
_____

Part 2

_____
_____
_____
_____
_____
_____
_____
_____
_____
_____
_____
_____
_____
_____
_____
_____

Name _____

Part 1

($ thousands)	2011	2010	2009
Total Revenue			
Off-Road Vehicles			
Snowmobiles			
On-Road Vehicles			
Parts, Garments & Accessories			

Part 2

_____

_____

_____

_____

_____

_____

_____

Part 3 FastForward

Total Revenue		
Off-Road Vehicles		
Snowmobiles		
On-Road Vehicles		
Parts, Garments & Accessories		

Part 1

Polaris's profit margin _____

_____

Arctic Cat's profit margin _____

_____

_____

Part 2

Polaris's investment turnover _____

_____

Arctic Cat's investment turnover _____

_____

_____

Part 3

_____

_____

_____

_____

_____

_____

(1) Identification of any Ethical Concern(s) _____

_____

_____

_____

_____

_____

_____

_____

_____

_____

_____

_____

_____

_____

(2) Action Plan to Eliminate or Reduce any Ethical Concern(s) _____

_____

_____

_____

_____

_____

_____

_____

_____

_____

_____

_____

_____

_____

(3) Identification of Empolyer's Ethical Responsibility(ies) _____

_____

_____

_____

_____

_____

_____

_____

_____

_____

_____

_____

MEMORANDUM

TO:
FROM:
SUBJECT: Explanation of Home Office Expense in performance report
DATE:

_____
_____
_____
_____
_____
_____
_____
_____
_____
_____
_____
_____
_____
_____
_____
_____
_____
_____
_____
_____
_____
_____
_____
_____
_____
_____
_____
_____

Part 1

| **Tutorial** | **Notes about Tutorial** |

(i) _____

_____

_____

_____

_____

(ii) _____

_____

_____

_____

_____

(iii) _____

_____

_____

_____

_____

MEMORANDUM

TO:

FROM:

SUBJECT: Applications useful in business and managerial decision making

DATE:

_____

_____

_____

_____

_____

_____

_____

_____

_____

_____

_____

_____

_____

_____

_____

_____

Part 1

_____
_____
_____
_____
_____
_____
_____
_____
_____
_____
_____
_____
_____
_____
_____
_____
_____
_____
_____

Part 2

_____
_____
_____
_____
_____
_____
_____
_____
_____
_____

(1) _____
_____
_____
_____
_____
_____

(2) _____
_____
_____
_____
_____
_____
_____

(3) _____
_____
_____
_____
_____
_____

Hitting the Road--BTN 24-8

(1) Recommendation to the Segment Departments for Responsibility Reporting _____
_____
_____
_____
_____
_____
_____

(2) Proposal for an Expense Allocation System

Expense	Allocation Base
Heat...........................	
Rent...........................	
Insurance..................	
Maintenance...............	

1.

   Net sales growth (in percent)

Segment	Net sales percent change from 20___ to 20___
Two-Wheeler...…………	
Commercial Vehicles…	

2. Identification of Fast-Growth Segment _____
_____
_____

3. Identification of Most Profitable Segment _____
_____
_____

4 Explanation of Management Use of Segment Information _____
_____
_____
_____
_____
_____
_____
_____
_____
_____

Payback Period _____

_____
_____
_____
_____
_____
_____
_____

Quick Study 25-2

(1) Identification of Preferred Investment _____

_____
_____

(2) Explanation of Why Investment B might be Preferred to Investment A _____

_____
_____
_____
_____
_____
_____
_____
_____

Quick Study 25-3

Accounting Rate of Return _____

_____
_____
_____
_____
_____
_____

Net Present Value

_____
_____
_____
_____
_____
_____
_____
_____
_____
_____
_____
_____

Quick Study 25-5

Profitability Index: _____
    Project A: _____
_____
    Project B: _____
_____

Interpretation: _____
_____
_____

Quick Study 25-6
Internal Rate of Return and Present Value Factor _____
_____
_____
_____
_____

Quick Study 25-7

1. _____
2. _____
3. _____
4. _____
5. _____

Incremental Cost Analysis

_____
_____
_____
_____
_____
_____
_____

Interpretation:

_____
_____

Quick Study 25-9

Most Profitable Sales Mix

_____
_____
_____
_____
_____
_____
_____
_____
_____

Quick Study 25-10

Incremental Revenue and Cost of Additional Processing

_____
_____
_____
_____
_____
_____

Incremental Revenue and Cost of Rework

_____
_____
_____
_____
_____
_____
_____

Quick Study 25-12

Incremental Income from New Business

_____
_____
_____
_____
_____
_____

Quick Study 25-13

	Avoidable Expenses	Unavoidable Expenses

Incremental Income from Replacing Machine _____

_____

_____

_____

_____

_____

_____

Quick Study 25-15

Year	Cash Flows	Present Value of 1 at ___%	Present value of cash flows	Cumulative present value of cash flows
0				
1				
2				
3				
4				
5				

Break-Even Time _____

_____

_____

_____

Quick Study 25-16

(1) Payback Period _____

_____

_____

_____

_____

(2) Net Present Value of Investment _____

_____

_____

_____

	Annual Net Cash flows	Cumulative Cash Flows
Year 1		
Year 2		
Year 3		
Year 4		
Year 5		

Payback Period _____

_____
_____
_____
_____

Exercise 25-2

	Net Income	Depreciation	Net Cash Flow	Cumulative Cash Flow
Year 1				
Year 2				
Year 3				
Year 4				
Year 5				

Payback Period _____

_____
_____
_____
_____
_____
_____
_____
_____

(a) Payback Period _____

_____

_____

_____

_____

_____

_____

_____

_____

(b) Payback Period _____

_____

_____

_____

_____

_____

_____

_____

Accounting Rate of Return

_____
_____
_____
_____
_____
_____
_____
_____

Exercise 25-5

	Net Income	Cash Flows
Sales		
Materials, labor & overhead		
Depreciation		
Selling and administrative		
Pretax income		
Income taxes		
Net income		
Net cash flows		

(1) Payback Period

_____
_____
_____
_____
_____
_____
_____
_____

(2) Accounting Rate of Return

_____
_____
_____
_____
_____
_____
_____
_____
_____

	Annual Net Cash Flows	Present Value of Annuity at __%	Present Value of Net Cash Flows
Years 1 through 6			
Amount invested			
Net present value of investment			

Acceptability of Investment _____

_____

_____

_____

Exercise 25-7

1.

Project C1

	Net Cash Flows	Present Value of 1 at __%	Present Value of Net Cash Flows
Year 1			
Year 2			
Year 3			
Totals			
Amount invested			
Net present value			

Project C2

	Net Cash Flows	Present Value of 1 at __%	Present Value of Net Cash Flows
Year 1			
Year 2			
Year 3			
Totals			
Amount invested			
Net present value			

Project C3

	Net Cash Flows	Present Value of 1 at __%	Present Value of Net Cash Flows
Year 1			
Year 2			
Year 3			
Totals			
Amount invested			
Net present value			

Analysis and interpretation:

_____

_____

_____

2. Internal Rate of Return vs. Net Present Value

_____

_____

_____

_____

3. Internal Rate of Return for C2

_____

_____

_____

_____

_____

Project A

	Net Cash Flows	Present Value of 1 at __%	Present Value of Net Cash Flows
Year 1			
Year 2			
Year 3			
Year 4			
Year 5			
Totals			
Amount invested			
Net present value			

Project B

	Net Cash Flows	Present Value of 1 at __%	Present Value of Net Cash Flows
Year 1			
Year 2			
Year 3			
Year 4			
Year 5			
Totals			
Amount invested			
Net present value			

Profitability Index:

Project A: _____

_____

Project B: _____

_____

Interpretation: _____

_____

_____

_____

	A	B	Project A C	Project B D
1	Initial investment			
2	Annual cash flows, end of period			
3		1		
4		2		
5		3		
6		4		
7		5		
8	Formula for IRR		=IRR(C1:C7)	=IRR(D1:D7)

Or Attach Excel Spreadsheet

Exercise 25-10

1. _____   4. _____
2. _____   5. _____
3. _____

Exercise 25-11

Alternative A: Increase (or Decrease) in Income _____

_____
_____
_____
_____
_____

Alternative B: Increase (or Decrease) in Income _____

_____
_____
_____
_____
_____

Name _____

1. _____

_____

2. Incremental Income from Rework _____

_____

_____

_____

3. _____

_____

Exercise 25-13

	Normal Volume	Additional Volume	Combined Total
Sales			
Costs and expenses			
Direct materials			
Direct labor			
Overhead			
Selling expenses			
Administrative expenses			
Total costs and expenses			
Net income			

Management Recommendation: _____

_____

_____

_____

Chapter 25   Exercise 25-14   *Name* _____

Incremental Cost of Making the Part:

_____
_____
_____
_____
_____
_____
_____
_____
_____

Incremental Cost of Buying the Part:

_____
_____
_____
_____
_____
_____
_____
_____
_____
_____

Management Recommendation:

_____
_____
_____
_____
_____

Incremental Revenue and Cost of Additional Processing: _____

_____

_____

_____

_____

_____

_____

_____

_____

_____

_____

_____

_____

_____

_____

_____

Management Recommendation: _____

_____

_____

_____

Exercise 25-16

(1) No Departments Eliminated:

	Total	M	N	O	P	T
Sales						
Expenses						
Avoidable						
Unavoidable						
Total expenses						
Net Income (loss)						

_____

_____

_____

_____

_____

(2) Departments with Expected Net Losses Eliminated:

	Total	M	N	O	P	T
Sales						
Expenses						
Avoidable						
Unavoidable						
Total expenses						
Net Income (loss)						

(3) Departments with Less Sales than Avoidable Expenses Eliminated:

	Total	M	N	O	P	T
Sales						
Expenses						
Avoidable						
Unavoidable						
Total expenses						
Net Income (loss)						

(1) Sales Mix Computations and Recommendation:

_____
_____
_____
_____
_____
_____
_____
_____
_____
_____
_____
_____
_____
_____
_____
_____
_____
_____
_____

(2) Contribution Margin from the Recommended Sales Mix:

_____
_____
_____
_____
_____
_____
_____
_____

(1) Recovery time for:

    Payback Period

_____

_____

_____

    Break-Even Time

_____

_____

_____

(2) Advantages of Break-Even time

_____

_____

_____

_____

_____

(3) Conditions Yielding Similar Results for Payback Period and Break-Even Time

_____

_____

_____

_____

_____

Part 1

Annual Straight-Line Depreciation _____

_____

_____

_____

_____

_____

Part 2

	Net Income	Net Cash Flow
Expected annual sales of new product		
Expected annual costs of new product		
Direct materials		
Direct labor		
Overhead excluding depr. on new asset		
Depreciation on new asset		
Selling and administrative expenses		
Income before taxes		
Income taxes		
Net income		
Net cash flow		

Computations: _____

_____

_____

_____

Part 3

Payback period _____

_____

_____

_____

_____

_____

Part 4

Accounting rate of return _____

_____
_____
_____
_____
_____
_____
_____
_____
_____

Part 5

	Net Cash Flows	Present Value of 1 at ____%	Present Value of Net Cash Flows
Year 1			
Year 2			
Year 3			
Year 4*			
Totals			
Amount invested			
Net present value			

*Year 4 includes the salvage value impact.

_____
_____
_____
_____
_____

Part 1

Project _____ **Net Cash Flow** _____

_____
_____
_____
_____
_____

Project _____ **Net Cash Flow** _____

_____
_____
_____
_____
_____
_____

Part 2

Project _____ **Payback Period** _____

_____
_____
_____
_____
_____

Project _____ **Payback Period** _____

_____
_____
_____
_____
_____
_____

Part 3

Project _____ Accounting Rate of Return

_____
_____
_____
_____
_____
_____

Project _____ Accounting Rate of Return

_____
_____
_____
_____
_____
_____
_____

Part 4

Project _____ Present Value of Net Cash Flows

	Net Cash Flows	Present Value of Annuity of 1 at ____%	Present Value of Net Cash Flows

Project _____ Present Value of Net Cash Flows

	Net Cash Flows	Present Value of Annuity of 1 at ____%	Present Value of Net Cash Flows

Part 5

Management Recommendation: _____

_____

_____

_____

_____

_____

_____

_____

_____

Problem 25-3A or 25-3B

Part 1 Results Using Straight-Line

	(a) Income Before Deprec.	(b) Straight-Line Deprec.	(c) Taxable Income (a) - (b)	(d) __% Income Taxes	(e) Net Cash Flows (a) - (d)
Year 1					
Year 2					
Year 3					
Year 4					
Year 5					
Year 6					

Part 2 Results Using MACRS

	(a) Income Before Deprec.	(b) MACRS Deprec.	(c) Taxable Income (a) - (b)	(d) __% Income Taxes	(e) Net Cash Flows (a) - (d)
Year 1					
Year 2					
Year 3					
Year 4					
Year 5					
Year 6					

Part 3 NPV Using Straight-Line

	Net Cash Flows	Present Value of 1 at ____ %	Present Value of Net Cash Flows
Year 1			
Year 2			
Year 3			
Year 4			
Year 5			
Year 6			
Totals			
Amount invested			
Net present value			

Part 4 NPV Using MACRS

	Net Cash Flows	Present Value of 1 at ____ %	Present Value of Net Cash Flows
Year 1			
Year 2			
Year 3			
Year 4			
Year 5			
Year 6			
Totals			
Amount invested			
Net present value			

Part 5

Explanation of MACRS Implications for NPV _____

_____

_____

_____

_____

_____

_____

_____

| | Comparative Income Statements | | |
	(1) Normal Volume	(2) New Business	(3) Combined
Sales			
Costs and expenses			
Direct materials			
Direct labor			
Overhead			
Selling expenses			
Administrative expenses			
Total costs & expenses			
Operating income			

Supporting calculations:

_____
_____
_____
_____
_____
_____
_____
_____
_____
_____
_____
_____
_____
_____
_____
_____
_____
_____
_____
_____
_____

Part 1

	Product_____	*Product _____*
Selling price per unit		
Variable costs per unit		
Contribution margin per unit		
Machine hours to produce 1 unit		
Contribution per machine hour (or Contribution/[Hours per unit])		

Part 2

Sales Mix Recommendation: _____

_____

_____

_____

_____

_____

_____

_____

_____

_____

Contribution Margin at Recommended Sales Mix: _____

_____

_____

_____

_____

_____

Sales Mix Recommendation with Second Shift: _____

_____
_____
_____
_____
_____
_____
_____
_____
_____
_____
_____
_____
_____
_____
_____
_____
_____
_____
_____

Contribution Margin at Recommended Sales Mix: _____

_____
_____
_____
_____
_____
_____
_____
_____
_____
_____

Management Decision: _____

_____
_____
_____
_____
_____
_____
_____
_____

Sales Mix Recommendation: _____

_____

_____

_____

_____

_____

_____

_____

_____

_____

_____

_____

_____

_____

_____

_____

_____

_____

_____

_____

Contribution Margin at Recommended Sales Mix: _____

_____

_____

_____

_____

_____

_____

_____

_____

_____

_____

_____

Management Decision: _____

_____

_____

_____

_____

_____

_____

_____

_____Company Analysis of Expenses under Elimination of Department_____	Total Expenses	Eliminated Expenses	Continuing Expenses
Cost of goods sold			
Direct expenses			
Advertising expense			
Store supplies used			
Depreciation of store equipment			
Allocated expenses			
Sales salaries			
Rent expense			
Bad debts expense			
Office salary expense			
Insurance expense			
Miscellaneous office expense			
Total expenses			

Supporting Computations:

_____
_____
_____
_____
_____
_____
_____
_____
_____

Part 2

_____Company Forecasted Annual Income Statement Under Plan to Eliminate Department_____

Part 3

_____Company Reconciliation of Combined Income with Forecasted Income	
Combined net income	$
Forecasted net income	$

Analysis and Recommendation: _____

_____

_____

_____

COMPUTING NET CASH FLOWS FROM NET INCOME

	Net income	Cash flows
Sales...	$ 375,000	$
Materials, labor & overhead.............................	(200,000)	
Depreciation..	(50,000)	
Selling and administrative...............................	(37,500)	
Pretax income..	87,500	
Income taxes (30%).....................................	(26,250)	
Net income...	$ 61,250	
Net cash flows...		$

1. Payback period

_____
_____
_____
_____
_____
_____
_____

2. Accounting rate of return

_____
_____
_____
_____
_____
_____
_____

Part 1

_____
_____
_____
_____
_____
_____
_____
_____
_____
_____
_____
_____
_____
_____
_____

Part 2—FastForward

_____
_____
_____
_____
_____
_____
_____
_____

Part 1

Identification and Cost of Advertising Space _____

_____

_____

_____

_____

_____

Part 2

Estimation of Additional Product Sales to Cover Advertising Cost _____

_____

_____

_____

_____

_____

_____

_____

_____

Part 3

MEMORANDUM
TO:
FROM:
SUBJECT: Effective Advertising for Product Mix Decisions
DATE:

Part 1

Present Value Computation

_____
_____
_____
_____
_____
_____
_____
_____

Part 2

Estimation Errors and Investment Project Evaluation

_____
_____
_____
_____
_____
_____
_____
_____
_____
_____
_____
_____
_____

MEMORANDUM

TO:

FROM:

DATE:

SUBJECT: Evaluating Capital Investment Opportunities

_____

_____

_____

_____

_____

_____

_____

_____

_____

_____

_____

_____

_____

_____

_____

_____

_____

_____

_____

_____

_____

_____

_____

_____

_____

_____

_____

_____

_____

_____

_____

_____

_____

_____

_____

_____

_____

_____

_____

_____

Part 1

_____
_____
_____
_____
_____
_____
_____
_____
_____

Part 2

_____
_____
_____
_____
_____
_____
_____
_____
_____
_____

Project Identification

_____
_____
_____
_____
_____
_____

Qualitative Factors in Management's Decision

_____
_____
_____
_____
_____
_____
_____
_____
_____
_____
_____
_____
_____
_____
_____
_____

Part 1

_____
_____
_____
_____
_____

Part 2

_____
_____
_____
_____
_____

Part 3

Advantages

_____
_____
_____
_____
_____
_____

Disadvantages

_____
_____
_____
_____
_____
_____

(1) Lease vs. Buy Decision: _____

_____

_____

_____

_____

_____

_____

_____

_____

_____

_____

_____

_____

_____

(2) Management Recommendation to Lease or Buy _____

_____

_____

_____

_____

_____

_____

Global Decision—BTN 25-9

Rationale of Sustainability Program _____

_____

_____

_____

_____

_____

_____

_____

_____

_____

_____

Appendix B   Quick Study B-1   *Name* _____

(1) _____

(2) _____

(3) _____

(4) _____

Quick Study B-2

Annual Rate of Interest _____

_____

_____

_____

Quick Study B-3

Years of Investment _____

_____

_____

_____

Quick Study B-4

Value of Investment _____

_____

_____

_____

Quick Study B-5

Cash Proceeds at Liquidation _____

_____

_____

_____

Quick Study B-6

Amount Willing to Pay for Project _____

_____

_____

_____

     Name _____

Ending Value of Investment Program

_____

_____

_____

_____

Exercise B-1

Years Until Payment

_____

_____

_____

_____

Exercise B-2

Rate of Interest to be Earned

_____

_____

_____

_____

Exercise B-3

Rate of Interest to be Earned

_____

_____

_____

_____

Exercise B-4

Number of Annual Payments to be Received

_____

_____

_____

_____

Exercise B-5

Rate of Interest to be Earned

_____

_____

_____

_____

Number of Annual Investments _____

_____
_____
_____

Exercise B-7

Cost (Present Value) of Automobile _____

_____
_____
_____
_____
_____

Exercise B-8

Cash Proceeds from Bond _____

_____
_____
_____
_____
_____
_____
_____

Exercise B-9

Present Value of Investment _____

_____
_____
_____

(1) _____

_____

_____

(2) _____

_____

_____

Exercise B-11

Amount Borrowed _____

_____

_____

_____

Exercise B-12

(a) _____

_____

_____

(b) _____

_____

_____

(c) _____

_____

_____

(d) _____

_____

_____

(e) _____

_____

_____

(f) _____

_____

_____

(g) _____

_____

_____

(1) First Annuity:

_____
_____
_____
_____
_____
_____
_____

Second Annuity:

_____
_____
_____
_____
_____
_____
_____

(2) First Annuity:

_____
_____
_____
_____

Second Annuity:

_____
_____
_____
_____
_____

Exercise B-14

(1) Present Value of Annuity

_____
_____
_____

(2) Present Value of Annuity

_____
_____
_____

(3) Present Value of Annuity

_____
_____
_____
_____

Appendix B   Exercise B-15   Name _____

Total Accumulated in the Account _____

_____
_____
_____
_____
_____

Exercise B-16

Total Accumulated in the Account _____

_____
_____
_____
_____
_____

Exercise B-17

Future Value of the Fund _____

_____
_____
_____

Exercise B-18

Future Value of Investment _____

_____
_____
_____

Exercise B-19

	Present or Future Value	*Single Amount or Annuity*	*Relevant Table*	*Interest Rate*	*Number of Periods*
(a)					
(b)					
(c)					
(d)					

(1) _____   (3) _____
(2) _____   (4) _____

Quick Study C-2

1. Plantwide Overhead Rate
_____
_____
_____

2. Assignment of Overhead to Fast and Standard Models
_____
_____
_____
_____
_____
_____
_____
_____
_____
_____
_____

Quick Study C-3

Activity	Expected Cost	Activity Driver	Activity Rate

Name _____

1.
Fast
_____
_____
_____
_____
_____
_____
_____
_____

Standard
_____
_____
_____
_____
_____
_____
_____
_____

Quick Study C-5

1. _____
_____
_____
_____

2. _____
_____
_____
_____

Appendix C   Quick Study C-6   *Name* _____

(1) _____   (3) _____
(2) _____   _____

Quick Study C-7

Overhead Allocation of Indirect Labor and Supplies _____

_____
_____
_____
_____
_____

Overhead Allocation of Rent, Utilities, General Office & Depreciation _____

_____
_____
_____
_____
_____

Total Overhead Allocation _____

_____
_____
_____

Quick Study C-8

Activity	Expected Cost	Activity Driver	Activity Rate

Part 1.

Activity	Expected Cost	Activity Driver	Activity Rate

Part 2.

	Standard	Deluxe
Activity 1		
Activity 2		
Activity 3		

Quick Study C-10
Total Overhead Allocated to Operating Department 1: _____

1. _____

_____

_____

Model 145

_____

_____

_____

Model 212

_____

_____

_____

_____

_____

2. Model 145

_____

_____

_____

Model 212

_____

_____

_____

_____

3. _____ **Model 145   Model 212**

_____

_____

_____

_____

_____

_____

1.

Components
  Changeover _____

_____

  Machining _____

_____

  Setups _____

_____

_____

Finishing
  Welding _____

_____

  Inspecting _____

_____

  Rework _____

_____

_____

Support
  Purchasing _____

_____

  Providing space & utilities _____

_____

_____

Continued on next page

	Model 145	Model 212
Changeover		
Machining		
Setups		
Welding		
Inspecting		
Rework		
Purchasing		
Space & Utilities		
Overhead Cost Per Unit		

2.

	Model 145	Model 212

3.

Appendix C   Exercise C-3   *Name* _____

1. Client Consultation
_____

_____

Drawings
_____

_____

Modeling
_____

_____

Supervision
_____

_____

Billing/Collection
_____

_____

_____

2. Client Consultation
_____

_____

Drawings
_____

_____

Modeling
_____

_____

Supervision
_____

_____

Billing/Collection
_____

_____

_____

Total cost of job
_____

_____

Name _____

1. Total direct labor hours:
   Product A: _____

_____

_____

   Product B: _____

_____

   Total direct labor hours _____

_____

   Plant-wide overhead rate: _____

_____

_____

	Product A	Product B
Direct Materials		
A.		
B.		
Direct Labor		
A.		
B.		
Overhead		
A.		
B.		
Manufacturing cost per unit		

2.

	Product A	Product B
Profit (loss) per unit		

3.

Overhead rates:

Machine setup		
Material handling		
Quality control		

	Product A	Product B
Direct Materials (from part 1)		
Direct Labor (from part 1)		
Overhead		
Machine setup		
A.		
B.		
Material handling		
A.		
B.		
Quality control		
A.		
B.		
Total manufacturing cost		
÷ Number of units		
Manufacturing cost per unit		

4.

	Product A	Product B
Profit (loss) per unit		

1. Assignment of overhead costs to the two products using ABC
Rounded edge

	Cost Driver	Cost per Driver Unit	Assigned Cost
Supervision……………………………..			
Machinery depreciation……………..…			
Line preparation………………………..			
Total overhead assigned……………..			

Squared edge

	Cost Driver	Cost per Driver Unit	Assigned Cost
Supervision……………………………..			
Machinery depreciation……………..…			
Line preparation………………………..			
Total overhead assigned……………..			

2. Average cost per foot of the two products

	Rounded edge	Squared edge
Direct materials……………..…………..		
Direct labor………………..……………		
Overhead (using ABC)………………..		
Total cost…………..…………………..		
Quantity produced……………………..		
Average cost per foot (ABC)………..		

3. _____

_____

_____

_____

_____

_____

_____

_____

_____

Appendix C   Exercise C-6   *Name* _____

Part 1

_____

_____

_____

Part 2

Determination of cost per driver unit

Cost Center	Cost	Driver	Cost per Driver
Professional salaries……………………..			
Patient services & supplies…..….……			
Building cost…....………………………			
Total costs…………………..……………..			

Part 3

Allocation of costs to the surgical departments using ABC

GENERAL SURGERY

	Cost Driver	Cost per Driver Unit	Allocated Cost
Professional salaries……………………..			
Patient services & supplies…..….……			
Building cost…....………………………			
Total ………………………………………………………………………..………………..			
Average cost per patient…………………………………………………………..……..			

Appendix C   Problem C-1A or C-1B   *Name* _____

1. Activity_____ _____

_____

   Activity_____ _____

_____

   Activity_____ _____

_____

   Activity_____ _____

_____

   Activity_____ _____

_____

   Activity_____ _____

_____

_____

	Product_____	Product_____
Activity_____		
Activity_____		
Activity_____		
Activity_____		
Activity_____		
Activity_____		
Product Cost		

2. _____ Product_____   Product_____

_____

_____

   Average cost per unit _____

3. **Profit per unit** _____

_____

_____

4. _____

_____

_____

1.

Activity_____ .... _____

Activity_____ .... _____

Activity_____ .... _____

Activity_____ .... _____

Activity_____ .... _____

2.

	Job_____	Job_____
Activity_____		
Activity_____		
Activity_____		
Activity_____		
Activity_____		
Total cost of job		

3.

	Job_____	Job_____
Average overhead cost per unit		

4.

  Activity_____.................................. _____
  Activity_____.................................. _____
  Activity_____.................................. _____
  Activity_____.................................. _____
  Activity_____.................................. _____
  Total.. _____
  ÷ direct labor hours................................. _____
  Per DLH.. _____

_____ Job _____   Job _____

_____

_____

_____

_____

_____

_____

_____

5. _____ Job _____   Job _____

_____

_____

_____

_____

_____

_____

_____

1. _____

_____

_____

_____

_____

_____

2. _____

_____

_____

_____

_____

_____

3. _____

_____

_____

_____

_____

_____

4. _____

_____

_____

_____

_____

_____

5. _____

_____

_____

_____

_____

_____

1. Plantwide rate: _____
   Engineering support _____
   Electricity _____
   Setup costs _____
   Total manufacturing overhead _____

_____
_____
_____
_____

	Product _____	Product _____
Direct materials per unit		
Direct labor per unit		
Manufacturing overhead per unit		
Total manufacturing cost per unit	_____	_____
	========	========

	Product _____	Product _____
Selling price per unit.................		
Manufacturing cost per unit.........		
Gross margin per unit.................		

2.

	Product _____	Product _____
Gross Margin per unit		
x Units purchased per customer		
Gross Margin per customer	_____	_____
	========	========
Total Customer Service cost		
÷ number of customers	_____	
Customer Service Cost per customer	_____	
	========	

_____
_____
_____

3. Engineering Support
   Electricity
   Setup

	Product _____	Product _____
Engineering support		
Electricity		
Setup		
Total overhead cost by product line	_____	_____
÷ Number of units		
Overhead cost per unit	_____	_____
Direct materials cost per unit		
Direct labor cost per unit	_____	_____
Total manufacturing cost per unit	_____	_____
Selling price per unit		
Total manufacturing cost per unit	_____	_____
Gross profit per unit	_____	_____

4.	Product _____	Product _____
Gross Margin per unit (from above)		
x units per customer (part 2)	_____	_____
Gross Margin per customer	_____	_____
Gross profit per customer		
- Service cost per customer (part 2)	_____	_____
Profit (loss) per customer	_____	_____

_____

_____

5. _____

_____

_____

_____

_____

Name _____

1. Plant wide rate: <u>**Total overhead**</u>   =
                            Total volume

	Product_____	Product_____
Overhead cost by product line:		
÷ Number of units produced	_____	_____
Overhead cost per unit	==========	==========

2. Total manufacturing cost per unit:
   Direct materials and direct labor
   Manufacturing overhead
   Total manufacturing cost per unit

3. Gross Profit per unit:
   Selling price per unit
   Manufacturing cost per unit _____ _____
   Gross profit (loss) per unit ========== ==========

_____
_____
_____
_____

4.

Activity_____	
Activity_____	
Activity_____	
Activity_____	
Activity_____	
Activity_____	
Activity_____	
Activity_____	
Activity_____	

	Product_____	Product_____
Activity_____		
Activity_____		
Activity_____		
Activity_____		
Activity_____		
Activity_____		
Activity_____		
Activity_____		
Activity_____		
Total overhead		
÷ units		
Overhead per unit		
DM and DL per unit		
Mfg. cost per unit		

5.

	Product_____	Product_____
Selling price per unit		
Manufacturing cost per unit	_____	_____
Gross profit per unit	_____	_____

_____

_____

_____

_____

6. _____

_____

_____

_____

_____

Part 1

Cost Center	Cost	Driver	Cost per Driver
Professional salaries			
Patient services and supplies (or Customer Supplies for 2B)			
Building cost			

Part 2

_____Service

Activity	Cost Driver	Cost per Driver Unit	Allocated Cost
Professional salaries	Hours		
Patient services and supplies (or Customer Supplies for 2B)			
Building cost	Sq. ft.		
Total			
Average cost per patient (or per customer for 2B)			

_____Service

Activity	Cost Driver	Cost per Driver Unit	Allocated Cost
Professional salaries	Hours		
Patient services and supplies (or Customer Supplies for 2B)			
Building cost	Sq. ft.		
Total			
Average cost per patient (or per customer for 2B)			

Part 3

Analysis of Alternative Cost Allocation

_____

_____

_____

_____

_____

_____

_____

_____

Name _____

1. Direct materials
   Direct labor
   Overhead (_____% of DL)   _____
   Total mfg. cost   _____

2. Setting up machines   _____
   Inspecting components   _____
   Providing utilities   _____

   Direct materials
   Direct labor
   Overhead:
      Setting up
      Inspecting
      Utilities   _____
   Total manufacturing cost   _____

3. _____
_____
_____
_____